3 Entertainments

Works for film and television

by Weldon Kees

Edited and introduced by James Reidel

KFS

NEWTON-LE-WILLOWS

Published in the United Kingdom in 2012
by The Knives Forks And Spoons Press,
122 Birley Street,
Newton-le-Willows,
Merseyside,
WA12 9UN.

ISBN 978-1-916590-04-5

Acknowledgements:

"Gadabout" and "The Waiting Room" first appeared in *The Battersea Review* and *em* respectively.

All photographs courtesy of James Reidel.

I thank Kathleen Rooney and Christina Verigan for their help in preparing this book for publication. — J.R.

Contents

3 Entertainments **is a selection** of late pieces and collaborations by the poet Weldon Kees. It includes two screen stories, one of which is incomplete, and a play for television written during the last two years of Kees's life. Used for my research in writing his biography, *Vanished Act* (2003), they are printed here for the first time to — yes — entertain and to suggest what they might have become as finished works. They should also be read for clues about Kees himself — his existence, how he tried to survive — and for how they might have changed the course that led to his disappearance, leaving his car parked near the Golden Gate Bridge in 1955.

That Weldon Kees became a poet could almost be seen as accidental given how much of his life came under the spell of Hollywood. Born in Beatrice, Nebraska in 1914, he grew up in the Silent and Talkie eras and spent much of his time at the town's two cinemas and reimagining what he saw there as puppet shows he put on with and for his friends. His first writings were movie reviews and gossip columns that he typed, stapled, and distributed to the neighborhood the way other children might sell lemonade. And young people from this part of southeastern Nebraska had succeeded in Hollywood, including Harold Lloyd and an older boy, whom Kees knew as Spangler Arlington Brugh, the actor Robert Taylor, who was already a leading man by the time Kees finished college in the mid-1930s.

Kees, however, did not become an actor. While he would go through life, with his trim mustache and lean good looks, being mistaken for one, he found his real talent in writing and began his career as an aspiring novelist instead. To support himself during the Depression, he, like many young people from his part of the Midwest, looked to Hollywood: where the film industry had plenty of work; where Kees surely saw himself working on scripts; and where literary men, given the examples of F. Scott Fitzgerald and William Faulkner, had only further enhanced their reputations. But, Kees's boyhood friend Robert Taylor refused to see him and the subculture of Hollywood disillusioned Kees enough to change the course of his career. Yet, as Kees became a poet he never abandoned the movies. His first published poem, "Subtitle," which begins his first book, *The Last Man* (1943), instructs the reader that his poetry should be imagined as a movie, specifically a film noir.

After stints with the Federal Writers Project and being a librarian in Denver, Colorado, in 1943 Kees moved to New York. There he did write for the movies — turning reviews for *Time* magazine and then newsreel scripts for Paramount News Service and later for the documentary filmmaker Louis de Rochemont. And, just as he did as a boy, he went to the movies. But, now he had hundreds of movie houses from which to choose and not just the fare produced in southern California. He met such independent filmmakers as Helena Levitt, whose collaborator, the poet and film critic James Agee, had befriended Kees when they both worked at *Time*. Indeed, New York City became a kind of accidental film school for Kees, as he picked up basic skills, such as: using a camera, cutting film, adding sound, and the like. Enough so that he contemplated producing a "new kind of documentary film" himself one day. Yet New York, like Hollywood, disappointed Kees. He was searching for an avant-garde scene that, to him, had not lost its innocence, that seemed spontaneous rather than cultivated for the careers of a chosen few, where he could be or refuse to be the poet, the painter he had become in New York, the sometime jazz pianist, the critic of books, movies, and art exhibits.

In late 1950, Kees and his wife Ann drove cross-country to San Francisco. There Kees continued to what could be called his "third way" solution to that conundrum American writers, especially poets, face triangulating such precious commodities as art, money, and time. If this suggests some iron laws, at least one can be attributed to that poet and amateur economist Ezra Pound in "Mr. Nixon," where he intones on those old, scratched Caedmon recordings: "And give up verse, my boy, / There's nothing in it." And that is the "first way," to find another line of work since there were and still are few openings for court poets. The second way? That would be academia in Kees's time. Yet, unlike Theodore Roethke, Howard Nemerov, and other friends, he could not see himself as a teacher. (The exception would be, perhaps, the poetry consultant to the Library of Congress, which Elizabeth Bishop held when she took Kees to see Pound at St. Elizabeth's. That sinecure is a rare example of the second-and-a-half way.) Indeed, his only finished novel was a satire about an English Department that he seems to have written in part to warn himself away. Thus, Kees never considered teaching in one of the many new writing programs that flourished after the Second World War. In San Francisco, he found *complementary* work that was conducive to his writing, art, and jazz — with the ideal vocation made easier when it took his many "transferable" skills and had the tools he needed, such as the cameras he borrowed to make films and photographs, as well as the most important one: time. Indeed, Kees learned to exploit the workplace from boyhood, when he wrote on the office typewriter of his father's hardware company. The third way for him owes much to this early play. That is why these three pieces can be read as part of a continuum for psychoanalysis as well as for Kees's showmanship.

For Kees, the third way had to offer the same existential freedom that San Francisco did. Whatever he did for a living needed to respond to all the existential course corrections, wrong moves and right, that he did when making art. Thus, each of the pieces here represent such moves as Kees approached his fortieth year and made a full circle, as if going back to when he tried to see Robert Taylor and was sent away. The irony, of course, is that Kees should have been set for life given his accomplishments. He had three books of poems, two published, and one in need of a publisher. He had a long string of short stories to his credit. He had written book, film, and art reviews for an A-list of liberal magazines. He could be counted as one of the Abstract Expressionists, and a gallery in New York City exhibited and sold his paintings and collages. He scored and played the music for the experimental film, *The Adventures of Jimmy* (1951), and photographed and scored his own contribution, *Hotel Apex* (1952), to the exciting new genre that Maya Deren and others had established. If he had made his new kind of documentary, it would have been this homage to a deserted building on the eve of its demolition, which is more collage than film. Even his "day job" now resonated with consequence. At Langley Porter Psychiatric Institute in San Francisco, he made data films and documentaries with the anthropologist Gregory Bateson. Kees took superb black-and-white photographs for the clinic's director, Dr. Jurgen Ruesch, with whom he would soon coauthor one of the first studies of nonverbal communication. Funding for these projects, however, from government and private sources, such as the Ford Foundation, had been dwindling, especially after Adlai Stevenson lost to Dwight D. Eisenhower in 1952. And the new Republican administration proved to be less interested in cybernetics and communication theory, and more into building the Interstate Highway System. Kees, too, would also have to weather the post-Korean War recession. For much of 1953, he had been writing music and lyrics with the clarinetist Bob Helm. Both hoped to create a new sound that fused the best elements of traditional jazz, popular music, and the bohemian, pre-Beat *Zeitgeist* of San Francisco.

Getting these songs published and making demo recordings was what Kees had in mind in July 1953, when he and his wife Ann stayed as guests at the Huntington Hartford Foundation, a Yaddo-like artist retreat in Los Angeles. Rather than write poems in one of the artist's cottages, Kees met his friend Nesuhi Ertegun, who had started a modest recording enterprise out of the shop he ran, Jazz Man Records, in Hollywood. Ertegun knew a lot about the music business and offered much advice to Kees, but Ertegun wanted Kees's help, too, and easily talked him into another venture — a spy movie set in Turkey, which owed much to Ertegun's background as the son of Münir Ertegün, that country's ambassador to the United States during the 1930s and early 1940s and one not a stranger to Hollywood himself for he had suppressed the making of Franz Werfel's novel of the Armenian Genocide, *The Forty Days of Musa Dagh* (1933), into a motion picture. The younger Ertegun knew a Turkish film producer trying to interest Douglas Fairbanks, Jr., in doing a picture in Istanbul based on the actor's success in the British film, *State Secret* (1950), which had been released in the United States as: *The Great Manhunt*. The producer just needed the right script. In a letter to his friend, Norris Getty, Kees, like some old Hollywood hand, wise to the ways of the studios, seemed pleased with the screen story that resulted, which is published here for the first time:

> We managed to dream up a 30-or-so page thriller a la Eric Ambler which I must say ought to make a picture even the most exacting can sit through. We even managed to ring a few changes on the chase-through-the-streets-of-Istanbul routine, and our false identity devices must be seen to be appreciated. If Fairbanks doesn't bite, perhaps we can sell it elsewhere . . . Hope something comes of this: cd. certainly use some moola at the moment to take care of my gambling debts, this month's payment on the Bentley, etc.

ASSIGNMENT TO PERIL

A point on the Turkish border, October 8, 1950. A line of refugees escaping from Soviet rule streams across the point of entry, and are cleared by officials. These are the last few moments before the border between Bulgaria and Turkey is to be closed by official Turkish action. The gates swing shut. Turkish soldiers guard the border. Some of the refugees that have been admitted look back and then march with relief toward Istanbul and freedom.

Some months later, in a classroom of a large Eastern university, Stephen Carraway, one of the outstanding American authorities on the Near East and a specialist on Turkish history and Byzantine art, is lecturing to one of his classes. He is a tall, handsome, distinguished man of forty-two, impeccably dressed and somewhat stiff and correct in manner. It is late Spring; the windows of the classroom are open; a warm breeze is blowing; the trees are in full leaf. As Carraway is concluding his lecture on Turkish foreign policy, a spectacled girl student, highly serious, raises her hand. Carraway recognizes her.

"Mr. Carraway," she asks, "what do you think was indicated by Turkey last Fall when she closed her borders and prevented refugees from the Iron Curtain countries from entering?"

Carraway pauses, glances out of the window and says, using his pointer on a map of the Balkans behind him: "If I correctly understand you, Miss Redford, the answer to your question is that the Soviets were taking advantage of Turkey's earlier policy and were planting spies inside Turkey. There is no question that Russian foreign agents came across the border along with thousands of genuine refugees from Bulgaria. This presented a real danger to Turkey, and the Turks had no other course of action but to seal up their borders to the East. During the last war, Turkey managed to stay neutral when every one of its frontiers was aflame. It took considerable doing. This recent move is still another intelligent step on the part of this coveted bridge between two worlds. Remember that Turkey is the main link in the Balkans in today's grave international tension."

The bell rings. As the class is filing out — and we see Miss Bedford look back at him with an expression of more than academic interest — Carraway's secretary comes hurriedly into the classroom.

"There's a long distance call for you, Dr. Carraway," she says.

Carraway looks up while gathering his lecture notes together.

"It's Washington," she goes on. "A Mr. Lingle from the State Department."[1]

In his office, Carraway talks on the phone.

"I wish you could be a little bit more specific about what you have in mind, Mr. Lingle," Carraway says.

We hear indistinguishable and excited noises from the receiver of the phone.

Carraway says: "No, I'm not teaching in the summer session, but I had planned to spend the Summer at Harvard working on my new book on sixth century mosaics."

More rasping from the receiver. Carraway's expression now shows decided interest. "Well, if *he* thinks it's important," Carraway says, "I suppose I'd better come up and discuss this with you."

More rasping from the receiver.

Carraway: "Very well, I'll take the plane tonight." Carraway puts the receiver down and runs his palm slowly down his face.

In Washington, Carraway goes up the steps of the State Department and is ushered into Lingle's office, where the two men greet each other. Mark Lingle is a highly urbane and persuasive man of about fifty. He asks Carraway to sit down, offers him a cigarette, which Carraway refuses. Carraway looks somewhat disapprovingly at the brand of cigarettes smoked by Lingle, and takes out a Turkish cigarette.

"Wouldn't you rather have one of these?" Carraway asks. Lingle puts his own cigarette down on the desk and takes one of Carraway's Turkish cigarettes and lights Carraway's and his own. Each of the men takes a long drag.

Lingle leans back in his chair and says, "I couldn't tell you over the phone, but we think we have located Carter Lee."

Carraway registers surprise. "I've always said he'd turn up sometime, even when everybody was saying he was dead."

The conversation, in which Carraway takes a decidedly rising interest, establishes the fact that Carter Lee, an American agent who was thought to have gone over to the Soviets in the late 1930's and dropped out of sight for many years, is now in Istanbul, having escaped across the Bulgarian border. Lee was reported to have been in Moscow in 1945 and, according to some reports, was being held prisoner; according to other reports, he had been shot; and according to still other information, had broken with the Soviets, completely disillusioned with them, and was attempting to get back to the United States with important information. This latter report has proved to be correct.

"Here's our problem," Lingle says. "Do you remember Ralph Manson?" Carraway shakes his head negatively.

"Manson," says Lingle, "is another American who was very friendly at one time with Lee in Europe when they were both Communists. Manson is still a Communist, and an important one. Our information is that Manson now has some sort of deep personal grudge against Lee, in addition to their political differences, and will do anything he can to keep Lee from coming back to this country. We also have pretty good reason to believe that the Soviets have allowed Manson to slip into Turkey and would not be at all displeased if Manson did away with Lee."

"What do you want me to do?" Carraway asks.

Lingle says, "We had hoped that you could take a plane tomorrow for Istanbul. We think you're the man to get Lee out of Turkey and return him safely back to us."

Carraway thinks for a minute, then he nods in agreement.

"Good. You are to register," says Lingle, "at the Park Hotel and wait for our contact there to get in touch with you. Our consul in Istanbul will help you in making arrangements when you succeed in reaching Lee. If you get into a real jam, get in touch with Zeki Altay, who knows about this situation."

"And who is he?" Carraway asks.

"Turkish secret police," says Lingle.

At La Guardia airport, Carraway goes up the ramp to his plane. He seats himself in a seat next to a window. He adjusts his trouser creases carefully and opens the current issue of *Foreign Affairs,* which he takes from its wrapper. He opens it and hurriedly turns to an article entitled 'Minority Problems in Asia Minor,' by Stephen Carraway, and starts to go through it with understandably close interest. He finds, with annoyance, a typographical error, and corrects it with a pencil.

We dissolve to Carraway turning a page of *Foreign Affairs.* Cut-ins of activity inside and outside plane: signalmen operating, other passengers coming up ramp, pilot at control.

Dissolve to Carraway turning another page of the magazine. He glances around as the motors are revving up, and looks out to see a very attractive brunette — about twenty-two, slender, vivacious, intelligent, running toward the plane. Carraway watches as she barely makes it into the plane and sits down in the seat next to him, the only vacant one left. The doors of the plane are closed. The props begin to turn over. The girl is out of breath. Carraway steals a glance at her. She is carrying several magazines and the one on top is another copy of the same issue of *Foreign Affairs.* There is an expression of mild surprise from Carraway. As the girl becomes aware that Carraway is reading *Foreign Affairs,* there is a guarded exchange of glances between Carraway and the girl.

The plane is now in flight. Both of them are now engrossed in reading *Foreign Affairs.* The girl glances to see which article Carraway is reading. They are both reading the same piece — his own.

The girl says, "Why, this isn't true at all! Any Turk on the street would know that the Lausanne Conference was signed in 1923."[2]

"Where do you see that?" Carraway asks.

The girl points to a page. Carraway puts his hand to his forehead and says, "It's a printer's error. I should have caught that when I read the proofs."

The girl exclaims, "You're Stephen Carraway?" Carraway acknowledges that he is.

On the flight it develops that she is Selma Eren, who is a native of Istanbul and has just received her M.A. in political science at Columbia. The ensuring scenes aboard the plane will bring out that she has a very alert, lively interest in current affairs, in contrast to Carraway's more academic attitude. She is a thoroughly emancipated Turkish girl — the days of the harem are over — and there is no question of her personal interest in Carraway, despite the fact that she twits him somewhat about his demeanor, which she finds too precise and unbending.[3]

At breakfast the next day, Carraway orders oatmeal — "I always have oatmeal for breakfast," — and shows a certain amount of pique when he is unable to get his favorite breakfast dish.

The girl finds this amusing. "Do you know what we have for breakfast in Turkey?" she asks. He shakes his head. "I thought you were an authority on Turkey," the girl says. "Don't you want to know what we have for breakfast in Turkey?"

Carraway: "I hope they have oatmeal there."

"For breakfast we have tea, olives, and goat's milk cheese." Carraway makes a face. Fade.

The plane is now flying over Balkan territory. Air views of the Dardanelles, Sea of Marmora, the Bosphorus, and approaches to Istanbul. Selma points out points of interest to Carraway. She informs him that her parents spend the summer at Büyük Ada, one of the islands near Istanbul, and gives Carraway her address there.[4] She tells him that she would like him to meet her father, who is a government official. Carraway says, "I expect to be very busy, but..."

The girl breaks in with, "Well, don't trouble yourself."

"I hope I won't be too busy," Carraway says. They are about to land.

At the airport, they say goodbye. A sinister-looking Turk watches him carefully as he leaves the airport. Carraway gets into a cab and we take him through the streets of Istanbul to the hotel, which is modern and luxurious.

Carraway signs the register and a bellboy escorts him to his rooms, which are high up and overlook the Bosphorus.

Carraway takes off his coat and vest, rolls up his sleeves, goes into the bathroom, and is washing and drying his hands as the telephone rings. He answers the phone; the line is dead. He hangs up and begins unpacking his bags. The phone rings again. Once more the line is dead. He jiggles the hook, gets the switchboard operator, and says, "Has anyone been trying to call me? This is Stephen Carraway in Room 905."

Cut to switchboard operator in lobby — an attractive girl in her late 20's, who says with somewhat deceptive sincerity, "I have no records of any calls for you, Mr. Carraway."

Carraway: "The phone has rung twice in the last few minutes and there's been no one on the line. Are you *sure* no one is trying to reach me?"

The operator says, "I would know if there had been any calls. I am sorry you were disturbed." Carraway is puzzled, walks to the window and looks out on the Bosphorus.

Face in on Carraway, in different clothes, pacing up and down in his room. A radio is playing Turkish music. He lights a cigarette and goes over to the phone. He starts to pick up the receiver, and then decides against it. He walks over to the table and leafs idly through a Turkish magazine. Finally he goes back to the phone, picks it up, and calls the operator.

Carraway: "I have to go out, but I want to make sure that if any messages come for me I will get them." He listens to her answer, frowning, thanks her, puts on his hat and goes out, locking the door to his room.

Dissolve to Carraway coming down steps of the hotel and getting into a taxi at the curb of the hotel. As he is closing the door of the cab, we cut to a young, muscular Turk who is leaning idly against the wall of the hotel, looking at a magazine with pictures of movie stars. He is wearing a peaked tweed cap characteristic of young Turkish athletic types. He is eating dried raisins by tossing them carefully into his mouth. He looks up, watches Carraway intently, puts the magazine in his pocket, and hurries to get into a small dark car. He follows Carraway's cab.

Carraway is seen next at St. Sofia, where a guard asks him to take off his shoes before entering, as is the custom in all mosques. Somewhat taken aback, but with gentility, Carraway takes off his shoes and enters the mosque.

Dissolve to Carraway looking at Byzantine mosaics. Carraway takes a small folding magnifying glass from his pocket and carefully examines one of the mosaics.

Dissolve to Carraway looking at other mosaics with magnifying glass. Close shot of hand tapping on Carraway's shoulder. He turns in alarm. A very old wrinkled Turk with a beard, very gentle in appearance, asks him in Turkish, "Do you know what time it is?"

Carraway looks at his watch and, in Turkish, with strong English accent, tells him the time. The little man thanks him and goes off. Carraway looks at him curiously.

Dissolve to Carraway in a restaurant eating shish kebab and rice. A small orchestra is playing native music. The man in the peaked cap waits outside the restaurant, reading his movie magazine.

Dissolve to Carraway in the Grand Bazaar. It is crowded and noisy. Venders are hawking their wares. Occasional one of them grabs at his arm, and Carraway breaks away.

Dissolve to Carraway looking at a vase in one of the stalls, examining it with care. A merchant is talking to him rapidly in Turkish, trying to make a sale. Carraway asks, in Turkish, what the price is. The man names a price. Carraway says, "Too much," in English and hands it back to him.

Dissolve to Carraway proceeding along the Bazaar. Merchants occasionally reach out for him and Carraway breaks away from them.

Dissolve to a closer shot of a Turk in a rug stall pulling at Carraway. Carraway pulls away, and then realizes that the man is pressing a piece of paper into his palm. Carraway uncrumples the note and reads it. The message is in Turkish, and we dissolve through to an English translation: "Dangerous to call you at hotel. Come to Gunes Sokak No. 183 in Beikos tonight at 8:30."[5]

The last numeral of the address is smeared, and Carraway peers at it closely to see if it is a 3 or 5. It could be either. He turns to look for the man who handed him the message, but there is another man in the rug stall smiling at him.

Carraway says, in Turkish, "Where is the man who gave me this note?" The Turk shrugs. Carraway asks, "Didn't you see a man who was here just now?" The man shrugs, shakes his head, but does not speak. Carraway resignedly glances at the message again, puts it in his pocket, and walks away. Fade out.

Dusk is beginning to fall. Carraway is talking to a policeman who is directing traffic. Carraway asks him for directions to get to Beikos. The policeman indicates the Galata Bridge with many boats docked beneath it, and says, "Take a boat."[6]

As Carraway walks down the street in the direction of the docks, we cut to the man in the peaked cap whom we previously saw at the hotel. He is now on foot and is following Carraway about a hundred feet away on the opposite side of the street. Occasionally he takes a raisin out of his pocket and pops it into his mouth. Carraway is unaware that he is being followed. The street is extremely crowded, with heavy end-of-day traffic over the bridge. Boats at the dock can be heard whistling; there are many traffic and street noises. Long shots in which we see both Carraway and the man shadowing him pushing their way through the crowds to the boat. Carraway asks an official which boat to take, and is directed.

The gangplanks on the boats crossing the Bosphorus at this point are narrow, somewhat wobbly, and their railings are flimsy. As Carraway steps on the gangplank and starts across it, a man pushes violently against him, whether by accident or intention it is impossible to tell. Carraway loses his footing and almost falls into the water, but manages to save himself by grabbing at the railing. When he looks up, the man who bumped into him says, "I am so sorry." Carraway gives him a look, and the gangplank is pulled in.

Carraway's pursuer leaps with ease across the short space between the dock and the boat. Carraway looks around and notices the man in the peaked cap for the first time.

Dissolve to Carraway leaning on the railing of the boat and watching it pull away from the shore. He looks out at the freighters and passenger liners anchored in the Bosphorus. The lights of the city begin to blink on as they cross, and there are silhouettes of mosques against the horizon. Cut to the man in the peaked cap, who stands some distance from Carraway, watching him intently as he tosses raisins into his mouth. Carraway turns suddenly and the eyes of the two men meet. The man eating raisins hastily looks away. Carraway's eyes narrow a little, and his brow wrinkles.

We follow Carraway as he walks up to the top deck. He leans against the railing with his back to the water, seemingly in thought, when suddenly there is the sound of a revolver shot. As Carraway looks up, a dead gull falls at this feet. There is a close shot of the dead seagull as the hand of the man in the peaked cap reaches out to pick it up. He smiles faintly at Carraway as he drops the body of the dead gull over the side of the boat. Fade.

At Beikos, the boat docks, and Carraway gets off. It is now dark.

Beikos is a small, quiet, residential town, and there is little activity on the streets at this hour. There is a sharp contrast between the quiet here and the activity of Istanbul proper. Under a corner street lamp, Carraway stops and looks at his watch. It is now 7:30. Carraway stops a passerby and asks him where he can get something to eat. The man shakes his head and says, "No restaurants around here."

At the newsstand Carraway stops and asks a newsboy where Gunes Sokak is. Newsboy directs him by pointing. "Where can I get something to eat?" Carraway asks. The boy points to a man across the street who is selling ears of roasted corn. Carraway frowns, but walks across the street and buys two ears of corn. We follow him walking down the street as he eats the corn.

The camera pans to show the man in the peaked cap who also buys several ears of corn and motions to the vender to speed up this transaction. A long shot in which both Carraway and his pursuer are shown walking along, some distance from each other, both eating corn. Carraway's first attitude toward the corn is one of reluctance, but he conveys, by the time he is on the second ear, that he finds it palatable enough.

When Carraway has almost finished eating his second ear of corn, he hears footsteps behind him, and turns suddenly. The man who has been following him pretends complete indifference to Carraway, and continues walking toward him. As the man in the peaked cap tries to pass Carraway, Carraway reaches out for him and asks in English, "What do you want?" The man shrugs his shoulders. Carraway repeats more insistently, in Turkish, "Are you following me? What are you trying to do, anyway?" The man in the peaked cap suddenly makes a break for it, and runs up the street. Carraway runs after him. The man in the peaked cap runs around a corner, with Carraway in pursuit, still holding his not quite finished ear of corn. Carraway turns the corner, but can see no sign of the man.

Long shot of a dark street, with one lighted café. Carraway runs toward the café and goes inside. He had entered a typical Turkish coffee house. People are playing cards and backgammon. There is considerable loud conversation. Some of the men are smoking water pipes with their distinctive gurgling sound. As Carraway bursts in the door of the café, all activity and talk cease as the customers look up at him. The only noise can now be heard is the gurgling of one of the water pipes, which an old man is smoking. Series of close-ups of faces looking curiously at Carraway.

A waiter is standing a short distance from Carraway, and Carraway asks him if he has seen a man with a peaked cap come into the restaurant. The waiter points to the back table and says in Turkish, "You mean that man? He just came in."

Shot of table in the rear where a man in a peaked cap is sitting with his back to Carraway. Carraway walks back to him and puts his hand on his shoulder. Close-up of man in peaked cap turning around. It is not the man who was following Carraway, but a meek, innocent-looking, and very young man. He looks up, frightened, at Carraway.

Everyone is watching Carraway now. It is very quiet. Suddenly the faces begin to show glimmers of amusement as Carraway stands holding the unfinished ear of corn. Carraway becomes aware that he is presenting a ridiculous appearance, and attempts to hide the ear of corn behind his back. This increases the amusement of the people in the coffee house. Carraway gets out of the coffee house as best he can.

Outside the café, he stands ruminatively for a moment, looks at the ear of corn with one bite still left on it, takes bite and throws ear away. He starts down the street again.

Quick dissolve of Carraway through increasingly dark streets. Carraway eventually pauses in a deserted district on Gunes Sokak, a street with only two houses. He is now in the country. Several dogs can be heard barking in the distance, and somewhere a cat meows plaintively. One of the houses is dark, and the other is brightly lighted. Carraway walks to the brightly lighted house and views the number, which is 185. He rings the doorbell. The door is opened by a dignified-looking butler. We see, in a brightly lighted living room, four very elderly men with stringed instruments, play a Brahms quartet. A very few other guests, all of whom are elderly, sit listening to the music. As the door is opened, the playing ceases and the musicians and guests look around curiously at Carraway, as though resenting this intrusion.

An elderly and very well-dressed woman in evening clothes emerges from the living room and comes to Carraway. Carraway says, in Turkish, "My name is Carraway," and looks at her. The woman puts up both hands, shrugs, and says, "Qu'est ce que voulez, monsieur?" Carraway says, "You were not expecting a Mr. Carraway?" The woman, who is most gracious, says in French, "No, but if you like chamber music, why don't you join us?" While they are talking, the musicians realize that the situation is being dealt with and begin the Brahms again. Carraway thanks the woman, apologizes, and goes over to the darkened house on the same street. This is 183.

He rings the bell, and we hear it ringing somewhere far inside the house. He waits. There is no answer. Carraway rings again. The camera swings away from Carraway and pans far down the street, where the man in the peaked cap is standing under a tree eating raisins, watching. A cat comes up and rubs itself against the man's leg, and he brusquely kicks it aside. The camera pans back to Carraway at the door, which is now being opened by a very old and wrinkled Turkish woman. Huge keys dangle from her belt. Carraway says in Turkish, "My name is Carraway," and waits for a reaction. Her face is mask-like. Carraway says in Turkish, "Wasn't someone here expecting me? Carraway. Carraway. My name is Carraway. American."

He pauses, because now, in an adjoining room, can be heard the faint sound of a voice chanting in Arabic. Carraway gently pushes the old woman aside and goes toward the sound of the chanting voice.

The door is slightly ajar. Carraway enters a room in which a man of about forty-five is sitting under a single lamp reading the Koran and counting the holy beads in the traditional Turkish fashion. The man looks up solemnly, closed the Koran, kisses the holy book, and places it on a table beside him.

"Mr. Carraway?" he asks.

Carraway nods. "Then I'm at the right place."

"Oh yes, Mr. Carraway."

"I think someone is following me," says Carraway. "Do you know who it might be?"

The man gets up from his chair and goes to the window and cautiously looks out. He says, "I see no one out there now."

"He was eating raisins, if that means anything," Carraway says. The other man says, "Come and sit down, Mr. Carraway. We have things to discuss."

Carraway sits down, lighting a cigarette. His host says, "If I may, may I see your identification papers?" Carraway produces them.

His host examines them, thanks him, returns them, and says, "Now, let's get down to business. My name is Muzaffer."

He starts to speak, but Carraway interrupts him, saying, "Do you know where Lee is?"

"We will talk about that," Muzaffer says. "It is not an easy situation. Lee has been here for quite some time now, but he is still a very frightened man. We will have to proceed with great care."

Muzaffer goes on to explain that at the time the border between Bulgaria and Turkey was open, he, Muzaffer, was one of the government officials in charge of the refugees. "Carter Lee was one of the last men to get across before the border was closed, dressed as a Bulgarian peasant. I must warn you, Mr. Carraway, that he is a most difficult man to deal with."

"Where is he now?" Carraway asks. Muzaffer says, "Just a minute, Mr. Carraway. You see, Carter Lee has been through a very great deal; he has been badly tortured, and his mind is in, shall we say, a very unsettled state. There is no question of his loyalty to your country, but there are days when he is so depressed that I fear he may take his own life, and there are other days when talks of nothing but of returning to the United States and making a new start. But his hopeful days are the infrequent ones."

"What do you know about a man named Ralph Manson?" Carraway asks.

"We have pretty good evidence that Manson also slipped across the border. Lee is convinced that Manson is out to kill him because Manson looks upon Lees not only as a renegade but as his personal enemy as well."[7]

"When do I get to see Lee?"

"Just a moment," says Muzaffer. He dials the phone and asks for a Dr. Ahmet . . . "Hello, this is Muzaffer. How is our patient?"

Sound of doctor's voice on the receiver.

Muzaffer shakes his head and says, "That's too bad. I am very sorry to hear it. Tomorrow perhaps? How long do you think? At least two days? Very well, I will be in touch with you."

He hangs up and turns to Carraway. "He has had a very bad day and is incoherent. I think it is best for me to get in touch with you. It will be safer that way — not to call you at the hotel. You understand?"

"Manson, you mean?"

"Exactly. You will receive a message from me in two or three days. Meanwhile you might relax and enjoy our city. There are many beautiful sights here."

We fade in on Carraway on the boat coming to the island of Büyük Ada. He disembarks. It is a beautiful and picturesque summer resort, with bathers on the beach and a lavish casino. There are no automobiles permitted, only horse-drawn carriages. Carraway hires a carriage, and gives the address Selma has given him. Her father's home is a large modern one, on a well-gardened estate. As Carraway alights, he sees Selma coming home from a horseback ride. She is surprised to see Carraway. They talk as they approach her father's house.

She asks him what points of interest in Istanbul he has seen so far. "Several places," he says, "especially Beikos. I saw a good deal in Beikos."

"What were you doing in Beikos?" she asks.

He says, "Well, I had to . . . I had to see a friend."

"To see about your oatmeal?" she asks. They laugh. Carraway's stiffness of manner has begun to give considerably.

She asks him if he would like to go to the yacht club on the island. He agrees. They dance, and she keeps asking him questions about what he is really doing in Turkey. He seems preoccupied and worried while they are dancing, and she comments upon this. Finally he admits that he has something on his mind, but is unable to discuss it. Selma says, "Look, I know Istanbul, I know the people, and if there is anything I can do, please tell me."

"You needn't worry. I'll work it out," says Carraway. "Sometimes," Selma says, "it is very useful to know someone whose knowledge of Turkey is not limited to reading about it." Carraway looks thoughtful.

We fade in on Carraway, in a change of clothes, entering the Sultan's Palace. This building is now a museum where many of the treasures of the Ottoman Empire are exhibited. Unobserved by Carraway, the man in the peaked cap watches him at a distance. A series of dissolve shots show Carraway looking at points of interest in the museum. He asks one of the attendants if there is a catalogue or guidebook to the collection. The guide directs him to the office. Carraway goes to the desk in the office where a pile of guidebooks is stacked. He picks up one on top and asks the price. The attendance behind the desk looks at him narrowly and says, "Oh, no, not that one; that is not the most recent edition, sir. Take this." She hands him one from under the counter. On the front cover is a message, "You aunt has moved to Yeni Sokak No. 68 in Sirkedgi, Room 12, and would love to see you at four o'clock." Carraway looks quizzically at the attendant, who is busily typing.

A street in an industrial section of Istanbul. Yeni Sokak No. 68 is the address of an old frame house with narrow dark stairways. Carraway goes in and after slight difficulty finds his way upstairs to Room 12. He knocks at the door. It is dark in the hall. The house is quiet, but Carraway can hear sounds as though furniture is being straightened. Then the door opens.

The man at the door is a heavyset, bearish, grizzled man with gray hair, about 48, with a close-cropped gray moustache. His clothes are disheveled and his hair is slightly mussed. His eyes are intelligent, cynical, and shifty. We do not see him clearly at first because of the poor light at the door.

"Carter Lee?" says Carraway.

The man scrutinizes Carraway carefully for several moments and then says almost reluctantly, "Yes, I am Carter Lee. Come in."

Carraway moves into the room and the grizzled man offers him a chair. The room is very barely furnished, with bare floors and blank walls. Carraway sits and watches the man as he paces up and down the room a few times.

"You have changed a great deal," Carraway observes.

The man turns and looks directly at Carraway and says, "Do you think so? The things I've been through in the last twenty years would change any man, Mr. Carraway."

"Oh, you know who I am?"

"Of course, Mr. Carraway. When I decided to return to America, I specified to the State Department that I would only deal with some disinterested outside person whom I felt I could trust. And of course everyone, Mr. Carraway, is aware of your reputation for integrity."

Carraway's face shows no emotion. "The last we had any word of you in the states was in 1945 when a New York journalist thought he saw you in Moscow."

"That is correct," says the other man. "I was being held a virtual prisoner there." He pauses, and then goes on, "But we are wasting our time. What I want to know is how soon can you get me out of here and back to the United States. Are you in a position to guarantee that the American authorities will be sympathetic to my case?"

"There is no question of it," Carraway says. "I have come here to assure you of that, and to bring you safely home."

"Home," the other man says, smiling faintly. "Yes. And how do you propose to get me out of here? Will we fly from Istanbul?"

Carraway's attitude seems to indicate a certain suspicion of this man's actual identity, but he does not reveal it to the man. Instead, he says, "Do you know where Ralph Manson is?"

"Oh, don't worry about Manson," the other replies. "I hear he is in a labor camp in Siberia — he's become a complete renegade against the Soviet Union."

"My information," says Carraway, "was that he was looking for you."

"I don't believe it," says the other.

"Very well," Carraway says, "Now, I'll need some information in order to get your passport from the American consul." Carraway takes out a notebook and pencil.

"Birthplace?"

"Philadelphia."

"Birth date?"

"August 20, 1903."

"Father's name?"

"John Gardner Lee."

"Mother's maiden name?"

"Elizabeth Carter."

This exchange is carried on in a very hurried, cursory fashion. The grizzled man's answers are glib and immediate.

Carraway says, "Do you have a recent photograph?"

The grizzled man shakes his head, smiling faintly. Carraway says, "Make an appointment for passport photograph first thing in the morning. I'll come to see you at this same time tomorrow." The man watches Carraway closely as he goes out

Dissolve to Carraway in a phone booth talking to Muzaffer. Carraway: "I got your message at the Museum and went to the address you gave me. Lee wasn't there. It was a man pretending to be Lee, and I'm almost sure it was Manson."

Cut to Muzaffer on the other end of the line, saying, "What sort of a looking man was he?" Carraway describes him. Muzaffer says, "That's Manson, all right. I think you'd better get in touch with Zeki Altay of the Turkish secret police."

Carraway: "What do you think has happened to Lee?"

"God knows. I hope Manson hasn't caught up with him."

In the office of Zeki Altay, a markedly intelligent, middle-aged official in dark business suit, Carraway is offered a chair. Zeki Altay calls a boy, who comes in immediately. "Would you like your coffee with or without sugar, Mr. Carraway?" Zeki asks.

Carraway says, "without, please."

Zeki says to the boy in Turkish, "Two, without."

After the coffee comes — and Carraway has made some polite comments on its excellence and has taken one of Zeki's cigarettes — Zeki informs him that he is aware of Carraway's mission. Carraway explains Lee's disappearance and the presence of Manson in the room where he was to meet Lee.

"It sounds altogether probable, Mr. Carraway," says Zeki, "that Manson almost caught up with Lee, but that Lee was watching for you and saw Manson from the street and made his escape before Manson was able to get to his room."

"Yes, that's what I thought might have happened," says Carraway.

"We'll see what can be done," says Zeki. "I'll get out a bulletin at once informing my men to be on the lookout for both Carter Lee and Manson."

We fade in on Carraway as he returns to his hotel. As he is going up the steps, a street urchin, about ten years old, comes up and hands him a message on a piece of paper. Carraway tips him. The message is signed by Carter Lee and asks him to come at once to an address across the Bosphorus.

It is beginning to get dark. Carraway glances quickly at his watch and hurries toward the docks. A passenger boat has just left the shore. An official tells Carraway that there will not be another boat for his destination for some time. A number of rowboats are drawn up on the shore and, in the darkness, Carraway approaches a man who is adjusting his oars and asks him if he will take him across to a point a little to the left of Beikos. Carraway cannot see the man's face clearly. The man agrees to row him across for a certain sum. Carraway asks the man to point out where they will land, which the man does. They climb into the boat and the man begins to row Carraway across.

It is very dark now. Occasionally searchlights and lights from passing boats briefly illuminate the oars and the side of the boat, but the oarsman's face remains in darkness. When they are about halfway across the Bosphorus, a bright light flashes suddenly across the oarsman's face. It is the face of the man who has been following Carraway. He no longer wears his peaked cap.

Carraway's face shows great alarm. The oarsman stops rowing, and with great deliberation pulls one of the oars out of its lock. He brings it up to bring it down on Carraway's head, but Carraway has jumped up and dives for him. There is a fight in the boat, which almost turns over several times. Carraway, with a powerful right, finally sends the man overboard. Carraway recovers the oar and starts rowing toward his destination.

He is very tired, wet, and breathless. Just as he has almost reached the other side, he hears a motorboat close behind him. Carraway makes it to the shore before the motorboat, jumps out, and we follow him as he runs through the streets, inquiring of several passersby the whereabouts of the address Lee has given him. As he comes in sight of this address, a man motions to him from a dark alley and pulls him into the shadows. This man is the real Carter Lee.

Lees's appearance is in marked contrast to that of Manson. He is of medium height, slender, emaciated, with fine features, and sensitive, haunted eyes. His hair is gray and he has a noticeable facial tic that seems to indicate continual physical pain.

"I waited for you here instead of at the house," Lee says quickly. "I was afraid Manson had got on my trail again."

"I think he's after me now," says Carraway. "What's the best way out of here?"

We follow Carraway and Lee as they cautiously make their way through the dark streets and along the shore. Lee is terrified of any sudden noise. After they have gone about a mile, a car with a spotlight goes slowly by, and they hide in an alley until it is out of sight. Making their way cautiously down dark streets and alleys, they eventually catch a boat leaving for Büyük Ada. On the boat Lee keeps repeating, "He'll kill me. He'll kill me. He'll never let me get out of here alive."

Carraway tries to assure him that he will be safe once they arrive at the place where they are going. "Tomorrow," Carraway says, "I'll get your papers at the Consulate and we'll get the first place out for New York."

"He'll kill me," Lee keeps saying. "You don't know Manson."

At Selma's home in Büyük Ada, her parents are away for the evening, and she hides them in an empty servant's room in one of the smaller buildings on the estate. Selma finds a sedative for Carter Lee, who is now near collapse, and Selma and Carraway get him to bed. When he has fallen asleep, Carraway thanks Selma and explains enough of the situation to satisfy her.

At breakfast the next morning, there is a scene with Selma's mother and father, Selma, Carraway, and Carter Lee. Her parents, though somewhat taken aback by the situation, convey by their attitude that there is nothing they can do with such a headstrong and willful daughter as Selma. Carter Lee is much improved after a night's sleep.

As breakfast is being served, Selma says playfully to Carraway, "I'm sorry I cannot offer you any oatmeal." He is served a large and traditional Turkish breakfast, and slowly and then smilingly indicates his approval of it. From this point on every vestige of stiffness is gone from Carraway's character.

A conversation ensues between Carter Lee, Carraway, and Selma's father which brings out their respective positions — Carraway as a lifelong adherent of democracy; Carter Lee as an American who turned his back on his country and then became completely disenchanted with Communism, and is once again fervently on the side of democratic methods; and Selma's father, a product of a new democracy.

After breakfast, Carraway prepares to leave for Istanbul to get a passport for Lee and pick up his things at the hotel. He needs a recent photograph of Lee for his passport. Selma has a Polaroid camera and takes a picture satisfactory for Carraway's purposes. A change comes over Lee — who during breakfast has been in an optimistic mood — while the pictures are being taken, and his eyes become glassy and frightened. Now all of his old misgivings seem to come back. He keeps repeating that it is useless for him to try to make the plane, that Manson is certain to catch up with him. He says that Manson will never let him get out of Istanbul alive. Carraway finally is able to convince Lee that the Turkish secret police have been alerted and that he will have their full protection. Lee reluctantly agrees to try to make a run for it.

To keep Lee in hiding as long as possible — Carraway has made inquiries about planes and is aiming for them to catch one at 5:00 o'clock — Selma aggress to bring Lee from the island later and meet Carraway at the airport at 4:30. Carraway says goodbye for the time being and leaves the house.

We fade in on Carraway concluding his arrangements at the United States Consulate for Lee's papers and plane tickets. Carraway returns to his hotel for his baggage. Playing it save, he takes a back entrance. A clock indicates that it is now 4:15. Carraway hurries up to his room and opens the door. Manson is sitting in a chair pointing a revolver at him.

"Just close the door quietly and sit down, Mr. Carraway. You are not leaving Istanbul just yet."

Carraway and Manson regard each other silently for several moments. "Where's Lee?" asks Manson.

"That's a piece of information you'll have to get from some other source," says Carraway. Carraway reaches in his pocket, and Manson motions with his gun for him to keep his hands down.

"I was just getting a cigarette," says Carraway.

"Have one of mine," Manson says. He extends a package of cigarettes to Carraway.

Carraway looks at them contemptuously. "I don't smoke that particular brand," he says.

"Oh, you don't smoke this brand?" Manson says, sneering. 'The time isn't very far off when you and a good many others are going to be smoking this brand and liking it."

"No, that's a very poor brand of tobacco that you have there, Mr. Manson," says Carraway. "And I think its popularity is due for a decline. And it's not too far off, either."

Manson takes one of his own cigarettes and lights it. He takes a long, pleased drag from it and looks up at Carraway. "Very satisfactory," says Manson. "And you'd be surprised how excellent they are, too, when the burning end is applied to the palm of the hand, or, shall we say, to a nostril.

Carraway looks at Manson contemptuously.

"All right, Mr. Carraway," Manson says after a moment. "This has been a very interesting little discussion of comparative tastes in tobacco. But right now I'd like to smoke you out on a matter of more pressing concern. Where do you have Carter Lee hidden away?"

The telephone rings. Carraway starts to get up, and Manson motions him back with his gun. The telephone rings again. Manson appears to be making some fast calculations.

"All right, Carraway," he says, "go ahead and answer it but don't say anything strange or try any heroics. I don't have any intention of killing you just yet, but I wouldn't mind at all blowing off a couple of those nicely manicured fingers." The phone rings again.

Carraway gets up and picks up the receiver. "Hello, Carraway," he says.

We cut to Selma, who is calling him from the airport. "Are you all right?" she says. "Did you have any trouble? It's getting late. It's after 4:30 now."

Carraway answers urbanely: "How very nice of you to call, Mrs. Bunn. But I'm afraid that tea *this* afternoon is quite out of the question."

Cut to Selma, who is saying, "Stephen, what are you talking about? You know the plane leaves at 5:00 o'clock. And Lees is in awful shape. He's — please, you must hurry! This is Selma, don't you know who this is?" Carraway says, "The oatmeal cookies do sound very tempting, Mrs. Bunn. You know how I love them. But I am rather tied up here at the moment. Rather tied up."

Manson says, behind him, "O.K., cut it short."

"Perhaps on my next visit, Mrs. Bunn," Carraway continues. "And do give my best to the Colonel."

As Carraway is hanging up, we cut to Selma, who is saying, "Stephen! What's the matter?" Then a look of comprehension comes over her face. She hurries out of the phone booth.

Cut to Manson, smiling grimly as he motions Carraway back into his chair. "O.K. Carraway," says Manson. "Let's spare the niceties. Where's Lee?"

"I don't know."

Manson lights another cigarette. "I had hoped I wouldn't have to resort to showing you my stock of cigarette tricks, Mr. Carraway. But then if one doesn't keep in practice one is apt to get a little rusty. Don't you agree, Mr. Carraway?"

Carraway can see Manson's wristwatch, its hands indicating 4:35. "What if I agree to take you to Lee?" says Carraway.

"That entirely depends on whether you actually take me to him or not. How far is it?"

"To one of the islands," Carraway says, "Büyük Ada."

"Oh, so that's where you took him last night? All right, let's get moving."

Manson keeps Carraway covered as he opens the door. Manson slides his hand with the gun into his coat pocket, keeping Carraway covered as they go out into the hallway.

Waiting for the elevator in the hall are four middle-aged American ladies, tourists of matronly size, two of whom are wearing fox fur pieces. They speak in hearty Middle-Western accents, and are chattering about the sights of Istanbul as Carraway and Manson come toward them.

"What's the matter with this thing?" one of them is saying impatiently as they come up. She wears a dress with a larger flowered pattern. "Some service. I'm just going to ring this bell again." She pushed it aggressively several times.

" . . . and then they served some of those heavy, syrupy doughnuts," one of the other ladies is saying. "They must have stomachs over here made of cast iron."

"All that olive oil," says another.

Manson and Carraway are right beside the ladies now. Carraway's eyes look toward the door to the stairway. Manson follows his glance. "Just watch it now," he says to Carraway in a low voice.

But the lady who remarked on the doughnuts has overheard Manson. She turns to him suddenly. "Oh, an American!" she says, overjoyed. "Isn't this nice! How long have *you* been here? The four of us are all over from Sioux Falls for a trip . . ."

Now the four ladies have pushed excitedly toward Manson, all of them talking at once. It is a moment made to order for Carraway, and he makes a dive for stairs. Manson pushes past the Sioux Falls contingent, bringing out his gun, but the door has already swung shut. Manson pushes it open and gives chase. The ladies are clucking like so many hens.

Carraway leaves the stairs on the floor below, runs out into the hallway, and heads for the back stairs. Manson is about twenty-five feet behind him now. On the chase down eight flights of back stairs, Carraway passes an open hamper of dirty towels and sheets, which he spills quickly across a landing. Manson shoots and misses Carraway. In getting past the hamper, one of Manson's feet becomes entangled in a sheet and he slips and falls. He picks himself up and continues the chase.

Carraway, arriving on the ground floor, takes a rear exit and heads for the street. A clock shows the time to be 4:40.

On the street, a Turkish youth parade is underway. It is a sizeable and colorful affair, with wrestlers, discus throwers, vaulters, runners, rowers, a band, etc. Carraway frantically pushes his way through the crowds that have formed to watch the parade and runs across the street through a group of athletes, who watch him in astonishment.

Manson does not see Carraway at first and stands on the sidewalk, panting heavily; then he sees him on the other side of the parade and takes up the pursuit. The chase on foot through the parade goes on for several blocks. At an intersection of streets, Carraway makes out Selma in her sports car, headed for the hotel, waiting for the parade to pass. Carraway runs toward her, motions her over to the other side of the seat, jumps in and quickly turns the car in the opposite direction, and races for the airport. Manson is seen hailing a cab and jumping into it, giving directions. Manson's cab gains ground on Selma's car, which has begun to develop carburetor trouble.

"Do you suppose he knows about the funicular?" Selma asks Carraway.

"I doubt it."

"Turn here."

They make it to Istanbul's famous underground subway, and abandon the car.[8] They get aboard one of the funicular cars just as it begins to move. Manson sees them from his cab and gives orders to his driver to go to the other end of the funicular line.

At the end of the line, there is as yet no sign of Manson. They hail a cab and make it to the airport. It is now 4:55. Muzaffer is there, waiting for them. Lee has reached a new pitch of fear and has locked himself in the men's room.

"You must hurry," Muzaffer says. "You have only a few minutes."

Carraway is checked through customs. "Goodbye, Selma," he says. He quickly kisses her. Carraway runs to the men's room and talks Lee into opening the door. Lee is trembling and ashen, and Carraway almost has to carry him aboard the plane.

"He'll get here," Lee keeps saying. "I've known from the beginning I'll never see the United States again. He'll kill me, he'll kill me."

"Nonsense," says Carraway. The plane is now warming up for the takeoff. "We'll be off the ground in seconds." He looks out at Muzaffer and Selma, who wave goodbye to him from the gate.

Just then, one of the airline's staff comes down the aisle of the plane.

"May I have your attention, please," he says. "There will be a delay of perhaps an hour. We find that the brakes require additional inspection. Needless to say, the company regrets this very much."

Total dismay on Carraway's part. Lee looks as though he is on the brink of collapse.

Then Carraway hears a shout from the crowd that is waiting for the plane's departure. Near Selma and Muzaffer, Zeki Altay and two policemen have a crestfallen and handcuffed Manson in custody. Carraway's face lights up, he nudges Lees, but Lee continues to stare blankly ahead as if all hope were gone. Finally Lee turns, and slowly his face lights up as he sees Manson can no longer harm him.

The official again comes down the aisle.

"We have another plane available now," he announces. He indicates its position on the field. "If you will all follow me, we shall be able to take off without further delay."

Lee and Carraway leave the plane with the other passengers and move toward the other plane. Muzaffer and Selma run out to greet them. Zeki Altay and his men can be seen leading Manson to a police car.

"Perhaps, Stephen, you'll come back to Istanbul again some day," Selma says to Carraway.

"Perhaps sooner than you think," says Carraway. They kiss.

Carraway and Lee climb aboard the plane and it takes off and soars across Europe, headed toward the Atlantic.

THE END

Notes

1. *Mr. Lingle,* Kees and Ertegun were close friends of the ragtime jazz pianist Paul Lingle (1902–1962), whose name is echoed here.

2. *Lausanne Conference,* a formal peace treaty to replace the one between the Ottoman Empire and the victorious Allies to end World War I. Kees is wrong here. The new Turkish government of Kemal Pasha refused to sign the new treaty.

3. *twits him somewhat,* to lightly reproach.

4. *Büyük Ada,* literally "big island" in Turkish and a wealthy district at one time inhabited by prosperous Greeks, Jews, Armenians, and Turks. Before his exile in Mexico, Leon Trotsky lived here for four years (1929–1933) after his deportation from the Soviet Union.

5. *Beikos,* i.e., Beykoz, an Istanbul suburb on the Anatolian side of the Dardanelles.

6. *Galata Bridge,* a famous bridge that spans the Golden Horn.

7. *personal enemy,* the conflict between Carter Lee and his nemesis Ralph Manson mirrors that of American communists who became estranged from the movement and those who remained loyal ("Stalinists"). This conflict had much influence over the political and cultural climate 1940s and 1950s and Kees draws on it here.

8. *Istanbul's famous underground subway,* i.e., the Tünel, the world's second-oldest subterranean urban rail line after the London Underground.

Douglas Fairbanks, Jr, did not make a movie in Istanbul. He went on to star in his own television show. Nesuhi Ertegun moved on, too, as his taste in jazz changed and he and his brother Ahmet established Atlantic Records. Had it been made, *Assignment to Peril* could have been developed into a kind of Turkish *Third Man,* even with its authors' touches left intact. One could easily imagine it running late at night to this day on the Turner Classic Movies channel with its dated, Cold War plot and the pedantic, oatmeal moody American scholar–hero teamed with a young, liberated, and secular Turkish woman.

Kees, too, abandoned the project for new ventures, from a music revue to a situation comedy titled *Helm's Hideaway,* about a jazz café starring Bob Helm as himself. Kees also worked on the manuscript of *Nonverbal Communication* (1956) and his long overdue book of verse, *Poems 1947–1954* (1954). His life, however, continued its unpredictable ups and downs. In July 1954, his wife, Ann Kees, suffered a mental breakdown while steadily drinking and watching the Army–McCarthy hearings on television. Prior to this episode, she had long been a high-functioning alcoholic and, although she eventually recovered, Kees divorced her thinking it would be best for both of them. However, he did so without realizing her importance to his own stability and his precarious sources of income.

To address the latter problem, Kees, together with a group that included the independent filmmaker Frank Stauffacher, founded San Francisco Films in the fall of 1954. It seemed a sound business decision. Columbia Pictures had announced an allocation of 10 million dollars to finance independent production of films to achieve the box office success of *On the Waterfront* (1954), slated to win numerous Academy Awards. The Theater Owners of America, at a convention held in November 1954, had authorized the formation of a corporation to be capitalized at a similar amount for financing independent productions. To get inside this waterfall of funding, Kees envisioned a wholly local film production company that would produce independent feature films, experimental films, and documentaries. San Francisco Films would also offer courses in filmmaking to paying students. The new company, however, never produced any movies, and the project came to an end with the threat of a lawsuit by Stauffacher's lawer, which prohibited Kees and his partners from screening the filmmaker's work after he fell ill with a brain tumor. Thus, San Francisco Films barely existed on paper. Where it did exist, though, for much of December 1954, was in the imaginations of Kees and another of his partners, the poet and novelist Vincent McHugh, who had once been a scriptwriter for Paramount Pictures, as they worked on the company's first screenplay.

Gadabout was to be a spy movie, taking its cues from the government's paranoia with Communist spy rings, especially in the aftermath of the Rosenbergs' trial and execution, and was to have the pace and gunplay of *The Big Heat* (1953). Set almost entirely on location in San Francisco, *Gadabout* featured an intrepid woman reporter, a manic-depressive scientist with a top secret to tell and a desire to be spirited out of the country. Much of the film drew on Kees's experiences working at Langley Porter and, possibly, on the clinic's complicity with the CIA and the clandestine LSD program known as MKULTRA. Written on a list of characters, among the three sequences that survive, is Kees's handwritten note:

Lysergic Acid = administered by phony psychiatrist

Weldon Kees (second from right) and the staff of San Francisco Films, late 1954.

Unlike the other entertainments in this book, *Gadabout* is not finished. It is, however, the only piece that was actually performed during Kees's lifetime: for what survives is a tape recording of Kees and McHugh brainstorming their film — made on the same machine that Kees used to record his radio program, *Behind the Movie Camera* for KPFA and other more outré projects, including his interviews with a ventriloquist dummy. If you can imagine hearing and transcripting their dialogue from the tape, both poets come close to performing *Gadabout*. One can almost hear in Kees's deep, Middle Western voice a desire to play the part of his *scientist maudit*, Helwig Ennis, whose personal demons are in keeping with those of a poet.

GADABOUT

All that survives of *Gadabout* are the working notes for three sequences and a nearly half-hour reel-to-reel recording of Weldon Kees and Vincent McHugh discussing scenes and characters. The latter captures not only Kees's passion for the project, but an occasional electric saw and or claw hammer in the background from a construction site near his Filbert Street apartment. One can also hear the meowing of Kees's cat "Lonesome," the clicking of drinking glasses, and the shuffling of paper as the two poets talk.

A synopsis is impossible to reconstruct from either fragment. The principle characters, however, extrapolated from working notes and lists, and the three typed sequences reveal the kind of film noir Kees and McHugh had in mind:

Martha Allen — a reporter for the *San Francisco Gazette*

Professor Bliss Culbert Allen — her father

Glen McBain — a CIA agent ("nuts about boats —/has friend in Sausalito/with")

Helwig Ennis, Ph.D. — a scientist who works in the Professor Allen's laboratory ("Hot jazz/liquors/dames/wife from whom he's separated/Several girl friend/Nurses/under psychiatric care")

Townsend Rudiger — an advertising executive from New York ("phony — smoothy/working a play for Marth/Lives in NY, on visit/Takes her to Place Pigalle/Algiers"); secret agent of a foreign power attempting to compromise Ennis

Charles E. Forward — Personnel Director of the research laboratory and GPU agent (Special Gaypayoo man — played straight/American — "That is correct")

Harry Peyrel — a private eye tailing Miss Allen ("Straight")

Ennis's psychiatrist

Friend of McBain with boat

Joe Dettrick — the street photographer

Sequence I

One point on the initial sequence when Martha is walking up to the Campanile[1] a hot rod crowded with hotrodders moves rapidly down the drive. A cat darts out in front of its headlights and the hotrodders swerve toward the cat to try to kill it. Martha goes over to the cat, but the cat is dead.

Sequence II

Martha pulls up in front of her apartment house in S.F. It is now roughly eleven thirty at night. Here, certain mood shooting of the upper parts of the old Victorian bldgs. Martha gets out of the car and we dissolve to her coming into her apt. She is greeted by her roommate, a divorcee of the Glenda Farrell type.[2]

The house has many cats in it, seven or eight cats. There is some dialogue of complaint about how the cats have been acting. She also tells Martha that during the evening there have been repeated phone calls from a man who left his name. He is from N.Y. and is called Townsend Rudiger. This name rings a bell to Martha, a knowledgeable newspaperwoman. However, she is most intent upon finding Ennis. The roommate also tells Martha that there was a ring at the bell only fifteen minutes ago, but she did not answer because she was afraid. At this point the telephone rings. Martha starts. The girlfriend answers it, says it's for you. Martha takes it. It's Rudiger, wanting her to go out with him and see the town.

We cut to Rudiger and introduce him in a telephone booth in a large hotel. He is in evening clothes and is a smoothie, a tassely golden Scott Fitzgerald type gone rotten. We cut back to Martha who agrees to go out with him and says she will be ready in half an hour. She hangs up. The roommate is getting ready for bed. Activity of cats. Martha petting cats. Martha thinks she hears a sound out in the street. She goes to window and draws the curtains. In front of the house a man is standing in darkness, a silhouette. As Martha looks down, his head turns and he looks up at her window. From far off the sound of fog horns and bells at sea. The man turns his head away and at that point a delivery truck, with "Flying Chopsui" painted on the side, pulls up. The man who has been standing there, picks up a basket containing dirty dishes and gets into the car. Conversation, very brief, between driver and man in Chinese. Very amused, good-natured, they drive off. Martha in close up, face expressing relief. She comes into the room feeling better, makes an affectionate gesture toward one of the cats. We cut back now as the camera with zoomar lens moves across st. and zooms up to a window of a house directly across from Martha's.[3] Seated at the window is a man only part of whose face can be seen. CUT.

Sequence III

Townsend Rudiger in taxi, pulls up in front of the house. Quick business of introductions, "Do you know this one?" "Oh, yes, of course I remember him." All that sort of thing. Quick dissolves. Conversation. Where would you like to go? She wants to go to jazz joints where she thinks she might possibly run into or pick up information on Ennis. He is all for hitting such places as Place Pigalle, Algiers and so forth. She wins the argument. Quick sequences. S.F. atmosphere, Telegraph Hill, Hangover [Club], Embarcadero joints, Pier 23, Blackhawk, ending with Martha and Townsend seated at a table at the Tin Angel.[4] Clancy Hayes with Scobey's band on bandstand.[5] Clancy sings theme tune, "Haunting." Cuts throughout Sequence III of Glenn McBain around, but not observed by Martha or Townsend; planted in such a way that audience has ambiguous relation to McBain. Is he on Martha's side or the people after the formula? At this point in the Tin Angel, after Clancy had completed his song, Martha talks to one of the waitresses who says that Ennis was in earlier and seemed in rocky shape. Said he might be back later. Martha, very tired. Townsend has to get up in the morning. Debatable whether to stay or not. Finally wait around for a while, but Ennis does not show. It is almost closing time. The waitresses are beginning to shake off the tablecloths and the musicians are getting bushed. They leave. They walk up the st. to hail a cab, and stand on the corner, waiting for a cab. Camera pans to the other side of the Embarcadero. We see a man, rather dumpy, 35, shambling, a bit drunk, across the street. He comes into the Tin Angel. The place is almost deserted. The musicians are putting away their instruments. He climbs up to the bar and the bartenders says, "How are you, Helwig?" Helwig looks at the bartender, and past the bartender, to his face in the mirror, and says, "Give me a double rye." The bartender says, "This is the last one." He pours him a drink, Helwig looks at the bartender and says, "Eddie, have you ever wanted to take the world and just," and at this point he cups his hands and presses them together. "Have you ever wanted to squeeze the world into a little tiny ball?" At a table behind, Chas. E. Forward is sitting, staring at the mirror. The light is reflected off his glasses — sinister.

Transcript of the *Gadabout* tape

Note: *Abrupt transitions in the conversation are denoted by em dashes; long pauses by ellipses; and bracketed notes are used for other conventions used in this transcription.*

Vincent McHugh: That might be best.

Weldon Kees: All right. Let's recap a little on that. Anyway, we do know that he's a very worried man. Somebody is putting the finger on him.

VM: This is Ennis?

WK: Ennis is a worried man. Somebody has the finger on him for dough. It's blackmail or some sort of squeeze. It's either —

VM: This happens after he leaves the laboratory.

WK: It's something that's been gathering weight, been taking on pressure for a long time.

VM: Yeah.

WK: He's had inklings.

VM: Or is he just the kind of *weakie* who wants something so badly that how he gets it won't — What would he want? What, to get away? Suppose he wanted to get away so badly —

WK: He can't get away. This is a security job. This is such a top security job, you know they won't let you quit.

VM: No. That's right. And you can't leave the country.

WK: And you can't leave the country.

VM: No.

WK: In a way his conflict is he has begun . . .

VM: But suppose he wants to leave the country and he wants to leave it so badly that he's willing to risk the security angle —

WK: That's right.

VM: — and if he's going to sell out the secret, he is certainly willing to risk the security angle.

WK: These guys can get him on a boat and get him to — across the Pacific in no time, if he just says the word. All he needs to do is write out this equation.

VM: That's why he wants to go. He wants to go to Tahiti or . . . some place less obvious, Port Moresby or —[6]

WK: That's right.

VM: — or, or Indonesia or —

WK: Or something like that. He doesn't want a —

VM: He's running away from himself.

WK: He just wants to take his . . .

VM: But that doesn't make too much sense.

WK: Well, it's better than some —

VM: It makes better psychological sense, but it doesn't make dramatic sense.

WK: It doesn't make dramatic sense. No. It would be better if there was somebody in Port Moresby that he's got to get to.

VM: I know a funny story about that. There was a guy who was in China with the Air Force during the war. A fellow I knew. And he said that he knew positively where there was Nationalist gold cached in the mountains —

WK: Hmmm.

VM: — that they've not been able to get to. He said if he could get a pack train in there, and that is the only way to get to it, he could get it even now. And his theory was that it might even be possible to bribe the Communist officials and get in there now.

WK: On the other hand, couldn't it, wouldn't it be, make better dramatic sense to have this guy wants something else? This guy really wants power. He's really jealous as hell of our girl's father. I mean, he'd like to take the credit for this. He's done most of the work. The old man is really a good scientist, but he doesn't —

VM: A coordinator.

WK: He's a coordinator. He doesn't have the genius that Ennis has. I think that's better.

VM: Yeah.

WK: But then we could have this scene, which we plant early in the picture, where we pick him up. And he goes into the Tin Angel, to hear some music, and he's talking, and he has a couple drinks and he gets a little out of hand, and he says to the bartender: "Did you ever have the feeling that you'd just like to take the whole world *and squeeze it to death?*"

VM: That's a good line. Yeah, yeah, that's a good line.

WK: And then the band picks up right after that.

VM: Hmm. Very good.

WK: Squeeze it in one ball, and you have, you pan the camera around, and Scobey is just picking up his trumpet, and he blows the introduction . . . to "Dippermouth."[7]

VM: Yeah.

WK: Something like that.

VM: Yeah, it's a very good line in the sense of . . . in the sense of a crushed-down resentment —

WK: We don't need Ennis in this scene.

VM: — aggressions.

WK: This is a short scene, which comes right after —

VM: What about this, Weldon? Let's face this right off.

WK: Yeah, sure.

VM: Do we stay on the girl's line or do we bat her out? This is your main problem, I mean in the story —

WK: In the girl's motivation?

VM: No, no. Do we stay with the girl all the time?

WK: Oh no, we can't do that. It makes for much too boring a picture —

VM: Oh?

WK: — if you stay with one person all of the time.

VM: Well?

WK: I think M . . . That was the trouble with M.[8]

VM: What about that one, that one Montgomery did, in which the audience — [9] ?

WK: It gets to be a drag. Your eye gets tired of looking. I don't care who it is. As far as movies go, you can't stay, you've got to keep cutting. You've got to keep cutting all the time. It makes for more fast moving stuff.

VM: Yeah, you've got to keep cutting.

WK: It makes for more excitement —

VM: Yeah.

WK: — and that way if you know where one person is all the time, you've lost something in terms of dramatic tension. You might as well do a stage play.

VM: *No,* I don't agree there. But I agree that you've got to have a lot of intercutting for this kind of thing.

WK: Oh, intercutting, yeah, of course.

VM: Yeah.

WK: But I think if you cut back and forth, I don't think you can stay with her all the time. After all, you can get something. The audience has got to know where *she* is part of the time. And the only way you can do it is to get away from her part of the time. The thing is — we're at Neiman's and talking about this — is we've got a divided business going on with her.[10] She's got two assignments: She's got her newspaper job, and she's got this assignment for the old man.

VM: Yeah.

WK: Now, I think what we better do is decide what's going to happen here. I — couldn't he say: "You're going on vacation day after tomorrow, aren't you?" or "tomorrow, and you can get on this for me?"

VM: Oh, but that removes our motivation for having her go to all sorts of places not connected with her, with her, uh . . . quest.

WK: I see.

VM: The spot at the beach, for example, she's going out there to take a look at the amusement park in the off-season.[11] See, she's walking along the seawall.

WK: Okay.

VM: Things like that.

WK: Did it stop you a little while?

VM: No.

WK: No?

VM: No, I —

WK: It's a good device.

VM: Yeah, because, after all, she wouldn't spend all her time at that, I mean —

WK: No.

VM: That's the role of the vacation thing, it would —

WK: Yeah.

VM: I got another gimmick there —

WK: Yeah.

VM: — which is very good, I think. She has a "futures file" . . . in the office.

WK: Yeah . . . She turns a card that says, uh, "Remember to, uh, remember to check the, uh, amusement park at the beach in the off-season." The gulls, the children, . . . all, all sorts of odd characters out there —

44

WK: That's right.

VM: See? Then she hits the odd — then we hit the odd characters. And the funhouse with the, with the really terrifying globbing figures walking around it, you see.

WK: That Norman Foster used —[12]

VM: Yeah.

WK: — yeah, in *Woman on the Beach,* and they used that an awful lot in that Hitchcock picture that Robert Walker was in.[13]

VM: There were some new rides, though, that we might be able to use.

WK: Some new rides, maybe, yeah.

VM: But the human grisliness of those figures —

WK: Oh yeah.

VM: Yeah.

WK: And we mustn't forget that windmill.[14] Nobody's ever used that windmill before.

VM: Right.

WK: And let's not forget the house down the street here with the turrets on it. She's got to —

VM: Oh, there's a wonderful theater on Polk, the Alhambra, with the lighted turrets at night.[15] Do you know that place?

WK: No. No I don't think I do.

VM: There's another point I thought of, just a tiny point, an audience identification point. Some of these foreign cars have three taillights in line —

WK: Yeah.

VM: — which makes a wonderful identification for her car. One, two, three, you know?

WK: Let's not forget. Did you jot down that business I had about going down to the — we get her down to the sports car races in Pebble Beach around about reel seven —

VM: Yeah.

WK: — and that's when our big chase starts. And we can get . . . go into a . . . I think a chase in that *beehive* down south. You know those tract houses where everything looks alike?

VM: Oh yeah, yeah.

WK: I think a chase around in that country would be wonderful. I don't think anything like that has ever been done.

VM: Where are these races? I remember now.

WK: There down at Pebble Beach, and that has some marvelous stuff down there. The windblown pines and —

VM: Yeah.

WK: — the woods down there, and movie stars' homes. Well, she could go down there to do a double assignment. She's going down there to check with Crosby and also covers the, uh, sports-car races.[16]

VM: Yeah, yeah. You might get her in the bocce ball court.

WK: Oh yeah, I think that's essential.

VM: And somebody tosses one of those balls. You know the way they toss them?

WK: Oh yeah.

VM: And just misses her.

WK: Uh-huh.

VM: Yeah. They, they are really kind of terrifying.

WK: Oh they are, sure.

VM: The way they toss them, they must toss them, oh, 75 yards, I guess.

WK: And as long as we've got these cats, could there be a scene one night when the cats get all out of line and there's a *hell* of a cat fight?

VM: Yeah, yeah.

WK: In the apartment.

VM: Well, they'll go wild if you leave them alone too long.

WK: Sure they will.

VM: They'll tear everything apart.

WK: Oh, I know what would work, Vince. There is this night when her roommate has a hell of a scene with one of her boyfriends. It's late at night, and our girl has come home from covering, uh, somebody at the Fairmont.[17] And she walks in on this fight between these two people, and this guy is slapping the girl, and this girl is hysterical, and the room is in great disorder, . . . and our girl, uh, is beginning to be aware that there is a man in this room across the street from her, and everything is squeeze play, and this guy that follows her around, Robert Ryan[18] — she's all mixed up with him and doesn't know whether she's in love with him or not, and she comes in and this fight starts, and the cats just go crazy, go crawling all over the room.

VM: Yeah, yeah, uh . . . What else did I think of there?

WK: Now, there's one switch, Vince. Robert Ryan — What's his name? Dean? —

VM: Dean. Yeah. Call him Dean.[19]

WK: Dean is the top secret agent from the foreign power, isn't he?

VM: No, uh, I wouldn't say so.

WK: I think I'd do that.

VM: No.

WK: Or she's got to think he is up until about the end of it.

VM: She may very well think there is something phony about him, yes. But, uh, I think that for our establishing of the real world outside her hallucinations, we must have him on the "square." The audience must, uh —

WK: — must identity with him —

VM: Yeah. I think so.

WK: — as some sort of symbol of dignity and trust.

VM: Yeah, yeah, I had that feeling anyhow . . . Now what about these other guys? Uh . . . what about the line of action for these foreign agents?

WK: They . . . have an inkling, not through Ennis, but through another line they've got.

VM: They know about Ennis?

WK: They know about Ennis is the man to get to. They know that Ennis is weak. Ennis' psychiatrist is a complete sellout to them. Ennis' psychiatrist is a guy who is on dope. He's a completely corrupt man. He's a guy who sleeps with his woman patients. He's a phony Freudian. There is a scene in which, uh, the psychiatrist, uh, I mean this Freudian analyst, uh, is having the pressure put on him to help somebody out, and he says, "It's $25 an hour with me, boys, that's the way I've always worked." He points up at the wall and here's a picture of Freud, and he says, "I got it straight from the master."

VM: Psychiatrists are going to think we had a bad time with somebody.

WK: Well, we can do something to indicate that all psychiatrists are not like this. This man is a — I wonder if Ralf Harolde is still around?[20] Do you remember him?

VM: No.

WK: God, he would just be masterly for this. He had a face that was so . . . *just right.*

VM: I got a pal, George Bennett, who would make a wonderful heavy.

WK: Really?

VM: He's an ex-Golden Gloves fighter and an ex-, uh, an ex-Navy chief.

WK: Uh-huh.

VM: And for a sapping job or anything like that, he really has practical experience.[21]

WK: Well, I think the head of, uh, the foreign powers, the secret agent, should be so smooth. I think he is a, a graduate of Princeton. Uh, he is just so nice to everybody.

VM: Here's a switch: suppose *he* is the guy who represents himself as the executive of a big advertising agency?

WK: She wants a job with him, maybe?

VM: No, but he's offering money to her for the secret. Money or whatever.

WK: But she doesn't have it.

VM: No, but he doesn't know that. And he thinks she can get it. Uh —

WK: — Well, that's it, Vince! Here's how we plan it! Dad says to her in the second or third sequence, whatever it is, episode, he gives her the letter he's written to his friend, and he says, "Will you mail this to me?" And we plant the idea that she's being watched during that, and they think that what Father has given to her is not a letter to mail, but . . . the actual formula.

VM: Yeah. In any case they feel that she's so close, they can . . . she probably knows about it. They can get it out of her. But the idea of the foreign agent guy, uh, being . . . impersonating the advertising executive, which is a perfectly plausible notion.

WK: But it's the same thing.

VM: Yeah, yeah.

WK: Two greatest kinds of cons in history.[22]

VM: The snowmen.[23]

WK: Yeah, the snowman.

VM: We must write a picture sometime called *The Snowmen*.

WK: (laughs) Well, in the sketch that Barbara and I are writing for the revue, the guy who is the agent for the singer of popular ballads is named "Snowdon."[24]

VM: How do you get the radio station into this? I haven't —

WK: Oh, that's easy. She goes to the radio station to cover — no, I would make that a television show.

VM: Yeah, but I'd like to keep it in KPFA.[25]

WK: Oh, at KPFA. I was thinking you could do a satire on a new TV show, and you have a real awful comic, somebody like Red Skelton, or even funnier would be one of these ukulele players with the Relaxol, and our advertising executive is very much interested in this show. [26] They might even use this comic as a way of getting messages to each other.

VM: Yeah.

WK: [Unintelligible]

VM: Yeah, of course that's a possibility.

WK: They say, "If so-and-so plays 'Yes Sir, That's My Baby' on the ukulele you know what that means, fellas"?

VM: We're in.

WK: Yeah.

VM: I like this advertising executive idea that you have.

WK: Oh, I think he's got to be there.

VM: Yeah. And then the other guy is, is straight goods, the personnel manager.

WK: Hm-hmm.

VM: But we don't know which is which. I mean the audience doesn't know which is —

WK: The advertising guy is awfully understanding, isn't he?

VM: Well, he's a, a big front man, but a very smooth, bland hand with women. Big expense account romance —

WK: Oh yes.

VM: — at the best places. Money's no object.

WK: That's right.

VM: In fact it's —

WK: Drives a Cadillac.

VM: Sure, sure. And he has —

WK: No, drives a . . . a Mark VII. [27]

VM: Does he? Well, this is a New York boy. Maybe he just goes around in a cab. I don't know, but . . . he's in form New York, see?

WK: But he has to be cast entirely different from the way they've been doing this sort of thing. Mankiewicz has an actor in, uh, in *The Barefoot Contessa,* and he was trying for one of these real cold millionaires, and the actor wasn't good enough. [28] I think I would like to see this man a little more silky. He's like, uh, *corn tassels.* That's his act.

VM: Oh, this guy is Princeton 1928.

WK: He's the golden boy. He's a completely corrupt Scott Fitzgerald.

VM: Yeah, yeah!

WK: That sort of thing.

VM: Yeah, this is a Scott Fitzgerald character *who survived* and went big.

WK: And went big, yeah.

VM: Yeah, and he's gathered no moss. I mean, he's a —

WK: From any side.

VM: No, he's really got polished on the way a little more.

WK: And he's the guy who really wants the power. I mean the kind of power Ennis wants — this man, our advertising man, do we have a name for him?

VM: Yeah, but how do we hook him up with the idea that —

WK: We've got to get him in fairly early in the picture.

VM: Yeah, but how do we hook him up with the idea, with the idea that this is the head of the foreign agents?

WK: Well, I think that can be . . . I don't think you need to plant it. I think you need to suggest it.

VM: His name is Townsend Rudiger.

WK: Oh yes, good ol' Townie. I think you do it through a —

VM: The private dick's name is Harry Peyrel.

WK: Uh-huh. How's that again?

VM: Harry Peyrel.

WK: It's too close to "payroll."

VM: Yeah, that's it. It's the French for "payroll."

WK: Can you pronounce it "pay-rell"?

VM: Yeah.

WK: Pay-rell, then it wouldn't be so poor.

VM: Sure, sure. Head coach is Rabbit Pullman.

WK: Uh-huh. Yeah.

VM: Two other laboratory technicians are S. B. Heiss and Russell Labnik. The girl's father is Professor Bliss Culburt Allen. . . . She's Hester Allen, Leslie Allen, Lispenard Allen —[29]

WK: Leslie's good.

VM: *Lispenard* . . . for a columnist.

WK: Leslie when it's a girl.

VM: Yeah.

WK: Has too much connotation with "lesbian."

VM: Yeah. Hester [unintelligible]?

WK: I don't like that either.

VM: Lispenard. Lispy.

WK: Not good.

VM: Yeah, a good girl's name, but not for her.

WK: Uh-uh.

VM: [Unintelligible.]

WK: Letchen?

VM: Joe Dettrick is the street photographer.

WK: The big problem now is in terms of cutting shifts . . . and I think the only way we can do that now, Vince, is to sit down and map it out à la Jamesian instructions of the big novels. We've got have a wheel or three or four wheels and start rotating them. And we've got to know where she is, where the boyfriend is, where Ennis is, where, uh, the advertising guy is. Those are people and the dick across the street. And I'd like to see one scene, which can be an awfully nice acting . . . assignment for a man, the dick across the street, after she has gone to bed, and he is waiting around for his relief, and he is just tired as hell doing nothing. He's got the radio on low. Maybe he's fixing himself a, a cheese sandwich and —

VM: — Is this the dick across the street in the apartment?

WK: Yeah, it's her father's dick.

VM: I thought this was the foreign agent.

WK: . . . *No,* she thinks that he is after her. But he really is the guy her father had put on to watch her because not only does he know she is pretty paranoid girl, he's got to have her help. But while he is away, he's got to have somebody looking out for her.

VM: Yeah.

WK: Because he knows, he knows, he's got inklings. Everything's been happening. He thinks his phone's tapped. It is tapped, of course, big security stuff. J. Edgar Hoover is listening in on him all the time.

VM: Sure.

WK: But in addition to that there are other inklings. I mean, he could have heard from Washington directly to watch out. That they know there's a risk. I think that's the way to do it. He's got to know very early in the picture, or tell her. He said, "Only yesterday, the reason I, uh, have to get to Washington so fast is that they're scared. They know there are people are people right here in San Francisco who are after this, and they think they know who they are. But, but you know, they don't . . . maybe they do and maybe even they . . . you know, the FBI will never give you a straight story." . . . Couldn't he say — does she see him off at the plane, Vince?

VM: Yeah.

WK: What do you want to do, play back?

VM: No, cut for a minute.

WK: Alright.

[Audible click at 21 minutes — the recorder is turned off — then the audible click of it being turned on again.]

WK: Yeah.

VM: Yeah, Ennis is traditionally well bred. He comes from a well-bred family, has the usual American ethical background, which is unpredictable lapses.

WK: He could go anywhere like Elder[30] did.

VM: Like the rest of us, yeah.

WK: Depending on what kind of woman he got mixed up with.

VM: Oh, I don't know about that . . . how far, how unethical he is, basically, in this way.

WK: I don't mean unethical. But he is a . . .

VM: Yeah.

WK: . . . a moody man, isn't he?

VM: Yeah, yeah. Unpredictable, let's say.

WK: Uh-huh. Now, if her father told her to see what she can find out about Ennis, wouldn't he say to her uh . . . Well, you know, what is Ennis's first name, Charlie?

VM: I've got it here somewhere. Let's see, uh, . . . where is it?

WK: You don't have a name like Monroe Ennis?

VM: Helwig Ennis.

WK: Helwig Ennis, yeah. You know how Helwig is. He's an unpredictable guy. And . . . you know the sort of places he's apt to hang out. One night may be he's down listening to Dave Brubeck. Another night he wants to get way off someplace and he's got that little place up in Corte Madera.[31]

VM: Yeah.

WK: And then he's been going up and down the coast a lot.

VM: And he hangs out in the Tenderloin.[32]

WK: He hangs out in the Tenderloin and he's all over.

VM: He gets [unintelligible] in bars.

WK: He has an ex-wife, doesn't he?

VM: She's after him.

WK: Who's on Telegraph Hill?

VM: She's after him for money.

WK: She's after him for everything.

VM: Yeah, yeah. Then, he's mixed up with girls.

WK: That's right. And once in a while — and then he's got this, uh, scientific friend of his who has gotten out of everything altogether who lives down in Monterey.

VM: Yeah, yeah. And just before the end, of course, Ennis is found dead.

WK: Oh, absolutely!

VM: [Unintelligible.]

WK: Absolutely!

VM: In the basement.

WK: From some very odd garroting maybe.

VM: And there are indications he's been tortured.

WK: Yeah.

VM: And the boyfriend[34] and the girl go to the morgue to identify him.

WK: Yes, yes.

VM: And then the last sequence takes off from that point.

WK: Uh-huh. Oh, couldn't her father say to her, "The one man, I think, who would know more than anyone else about where Helwig might be is his psychiatrist. But he has never — I know he is going to a psychiatrist, but I don't know who this psychiatrist is . . . "

VM: Yes. I've got this sequence on Ennis . . . the one about the . . . the street photographer.

WK: Oh yeah.

VM: I'll read you that one.

WK: Let's have it.

VM: Ocean walk on the beach, along the wall in the fog.[35] The street photographer takes her picture, offers it. She shakes her head walking slowly past. He thanks her. As she passes him, he, unmoving, without turning his head, says, "You look sad. Your face is crying like *the gods*." She stops. He half turns to her. She asks for the card. He gives it to her and tells her how to fill it out. While she is writings, she says, "You frightened me. You look like death coming out of the fog." He says in the same tone, "That's because you had death in your eye. No. I'm not death. I am life. I am a repository of life. Everybody pours his life all over me." She has turned toward the wall writing on it. He turns wit her. "Everybody's afraid. You're afraid. What are you afraid of?" She pays him, takes the receipt, says without looking at him: "I think somebody is following me." He looks as if he had not heard. They both look toward a man down the walk, leaning on the wall, just at the edge of vision in the fog. Cameraman says, "Go up the hill and wait for me at the Chinese idol. Ten minutes." She touches his arm, "You won't get hurt?" Without looking at her, he says, "I won't get hurt. Do you know who I am? I'm the last free man left in the world."

WK: Hmm-hmmm. Yeah!

VM: The camera follows her up the long slope to Cliff House[36] to where her car is parked. She waits beside the idol's bulging belly.[37] A man passes her, goes up the walk a little way. She puts money in the box for crippled children, rubs the idol's belly, then looks around half self-consciously, half apprehensively. The man who has passed her is watching

59

from the doorway of one of the shops above. The photographer comes strolling up the hill, cap pushed back, some cards in his hand. He takes her arm, leading her into the bar, stops, says, "You don't mind?" — indicating his gear. She shakes her head smiling. He takes his cap off, unstraps the camera, sits down with her, holds the cards out. He has taken pictures of the next five people who came along after her. She offers to buy them. He says, "No, you'll get the pictures." He says, "Number one-oh-oh-seven-three-two, middle-aged dark man, looks like a Hungarian, Magyar of some kind, about forty-five, uh, he has a crushed ear, his right ear —

WK: Hmm-hmmm.

VM: — as if with a heavy blow. Number two — and she — and he describes number two. Number three, woman with a baby carriage. Number four . . . as he begins to describe number four, uh, she realizes that it's Ennis. She sits up tense. He goes on describing him. She says — the photographer says, "He's the only one who bought. I've got his name and address." He shows her the card.

WK: Fine!

VM: The card says Helwig Ennis and gives an address out in the Sunset District.[38]

WK: Uh-huh.

VM: He says the fifth — he hasn't moved his head at all, he hasn't seemed to be looking anywhere — he says the fifth is outside the window looking at you.

WK: Fine. Now I've got something.

VM: Now wait! She looks —

WK: Yeah.

VM: — and it's the boyfriend. She starts half out of the seat to speak to him, to call him. He turns, gets into a car, and drives off toward town.

WK: Fine.

VM: So . . . they go to the home of the fourth man.

WK: Hmm-hmmm.

VM: They find the address in the Sunset. One of those houses like every other house out there.[39]

WK: Sure.

VM: They kind of walk around casually. They try the back door, the cellar door. It's open. They walk in and hide in the front room. After a while, a car comes up the drive. A man gets out, walks up the front steps, opens the door with his key, and walks in. And when he gets inside and turns on the light, he takes a bottle out of a cupboard, pours himself a drink, has the drink in his hand. And she gets up and says, "Helwig." He drops the drink and has a gun out of shoulder holster like that.

WK: Hmm-hmmm.

VM: He says nothing. The photographer is on his feet too by that time, walking toward him. He says nothing, backs out the back door into the car, [unintelligible] and out.

WK: Good. Now, we need to plant Helwig earlier . . . after . . . after she . . . uh . . . comes home. You know the scene where we have the two men out in the street.

VM: Yeah.

WK: There should be — we cut away to just a guy in a car. This is Helwig. And he is racing up the road in his car towards, on the highway . . . [Tape ends.]

Notes

1. *Campanile,* i.e., the Sather Tower, a bell and clock tower, on the campus of the University of California–Berkeley. Kees, in the weeks before is disappearance in July 1955, had contemplated jumping off the Sather Tower, a well- known suicide point.

2. *Glenda Farrell type,* Glenda Farrell (1904–1971) personified the wise- cracking, hard-boiled, dizzy blonde of the early talkies.

3. *zoomar,* i.e., the Zoomar lens invented by Dr. Frank G. Back f o r use with a 16 mm movie camera. Zoomar zoom lenses were later adapted for early television cameras. This hints how Kees intended to photograph this film using what was then the equivalent of handheld cameras.

4. *Place Pigalle, . . . Tin Angel,* all well-known San Francisco nightclubs, bars, restaurants, as well as districts known for their nightlife and demimonde.

5. *Clancy Hayes with Scobey's band,* Bob Scobey (1916–1963) and his Frisco Jazz Band featured not only his trumpet playing but the banjo and vocals of Clancy Hayes (1908–1972).

6. Capital of Papua, New Guinea.

7. *Dippermouth,* Dixieland standard by King Oliver's Creole Jazz Band.

8. *M,* i.e., *Dial M for Murder* (1954), a film directed by Alfred Hitchcock and starring Ray Milland, Grace Kelly, and Robert Cummings.

9. *Montgomery,* i.e., Robert Montgomery (1904–1981), actor and director. The film referenced here is *Ride the Pink Horse* (1947).

10. *Neiman's,* Kees interjects this, to remind McHugh where they are in the basic narrative.

11. *amusement park in the off season,* Playland by the Beach, the seaside amusement park that once occupied a ten-acre site next to Ocean Beach on San Francisco's far west side.

12. *Norman Foster* (1903–1976), film director.

13. *Woman on the Beach . . . Hitchcock picture,* Kees alludes to two film noir motion pictures, *Woman on the Run* (1950), a starring Ann Sheridan and Dennis O'Keefe, and *Strangers on a Train* (1951), based on Patricia Highsmith's novel.

14. *windmill,* one of the two massive Dutch-style windmills in Golden Gate Park.

15. *Alhambra,* a San Francisco landmark movie. Kees refers to its Moorish towers.

16. *Crosby,* i.e., in regard to the golf tournament hosted by Bing Crosby, which is the forerunner of the Pebble Beach National Pro-Am.

17. *Fairmont,* a luxury hotel at 950 Mason Street, atop Nob Hill.

18. *Robert Ryan* (1909–1963), a film actor who performed in noir pictures that Kees admired, which is why he imagines Ryan in this role.

19. *Call him Dean,* WK means the Townsend Rudiger character.

20. *Ralf Harolde* (1899–1974), character actor.

21. *sapping job,* to beat someone up with blackjack and the like.

22. *two greatest cons,* i.e., espionage and advertising.

23. *snowmen,* admen, PR men, and the like, derived from the term *snow job.*

24. *Barbara* and I . . ., i.e., Barbara Brockway, one of Kees's collaborators on yet another venture, a sitcom-revue for television titled *Helm's Hideway*, starring Kees's friend and music collaborator, clarinetist Bob Helm.

25. *KPFA,* call letters of San Francisco's progressive community radio station.

26. *Relaxol,* over-the-counter laxative.

27. *Mark VII,* Jaguar luxury sports sedan produced between 1950 and 1956. It was equipped with the engine from the XK120 and could reach speeds of 101 mph. It was the kind of car that appealed to Kees.

28. *Mankiewicz* . . . *The Barefoot Contessa,* i.e., Joseph Mankiewicz (1909– 1993), who directed the 1954 film starring Humphrey Bogart and Ava Gardner.

29. *Lispenard,* McHugh uses a French pronunciation of this name, which is more commonly a surname (possibly inspired by the street in New York's Greenwich Village, where McHugh lived in the 1940s).

30. *Elder,* i.e., Donald Elder, a senior editor at Doubleday who knew Kees in New York.

31. *Corte Madera,* a town in rural Marin County.

32. *Tenderloin,* part of downtown San Francisco known for its vice, including burlesque theaters, strip clubs, and seedy bars.

33. *Telegraph Hill,* a San Francisco district north of downtown and a bohemian and intellectual enclave not unlike New York's Greenwich Village.

34. *boyfriend,* i.e., Joe Dettrick, the street photographer.

35. *Ocean walk* . . . , this sequence takes place on Ocean Beach, at the western edge of San Francisco, the site of an amusement park as well as other attractions.

36. *Cliff House,* landmark San Francisco restaurant perched on the headland above the cliffs just north of Ocean Beach.

37. *She waits beside the idol's bulging belly,* a statue of the Chinese god Budai, a former tourist attraction.

38. *Sunset District,* San Francisco's west side.

39. *One of those houses like every other house . . . ,* a reference to the tract housing that is common in the Sunset District.

Kees set aside *Gadabout* to direct and produce the *Poets' Follies of 1955,* a fusion of burlesque, theater, music, and poetry in one revue. The antecedents for such a project had been growing in him throughout the previous year. How unserious it all sounded — an enormous antic, the kind San Francisco's bohemia loved. The production came together with the help of friends and contributors, including a troupe of Bay Area actors called the Interplayers. The *Follies,* too, should also be seen as part of Kees's third way of support — he counted on its ticket sales — but also as a kind of ultimate metamorphosis in which he could even abandon poetry — telling one friend he was "tired of that particular struggle" — for a career as a cultural impresario. After the show ran several times before closing in the early spring, Kees began writing a play at the end of April for three of the women he had befriended during the *Poets Follies.*

The Waiting Room has little in common with the screen stories. Yet *Gadabout* has a female heroine and *The Waiting Room* is a women's play. After the show ran several times before closing in the early spring, Kees began writing a play at the end of April for three of the women he had befriended during the *Poets' Follies.* Although *The Waiting Room* has little in common with the screen stories, one can see his feminist sympathies evolve across all three pieces to where *The Waiting Room* is entirely from the perspective of women damaged in some way by men — this from a man coming off a calculated, even coldly won divorce and an unhappy love affair with another alcoholic woman soon after (a similar empathy comes across in his torch song lyrics from this time and late poems, such as "The Musician's Wife").

Kees initially intended the play for the stage of the Showplace, a barn-shaped structure on Folsom Street in San Francisco's Mission District, a former boy's club and, allegedly, a music hall in the Barbary Coast days. Kees hoped to revive the space as a theater and art gallery, and, with the last of his personal funds, he leased the building for $60 a month. The three women who would perform *The Waiting Room,* Penny Vieregge, Jan Davis, and Nina Boas, helped with preparing the space, which was certainly used for its rehearsals.

Nina was Kees's favorite of the three. A petite, attractive woman in her early twenties with long dark hair tied in a ponytail, she was a painter as well as an amateur actor. She had even collaborated

The interior (above) and exterior (below) of Weldon Kees's Showplace, May 1955.

with Kees in developing her role as Nancy, a disturbed young woman. Where a pantomime scene was left unfinished, Kees typed on his director's copy: "QUICK BUSINESS TO BE WORKED OUT WITH NINA." But, unlike the more available women among the Interplayers, Nina had a troubled marriage to an eye surgeon and Kees himself was dating a psychiatrist at Langley Porter. He could only work with Nina in their rehearsals and read-throughs, during which, he observed, " She does everything but fly a kite."

The Waiting Room is not a long play. It was to be part of a program titled *Four Times One,* which initially included three other one-act plays: *Sweeney Agonistes* by T. S. Eliot, which Kees felt excused Eliot's religio-verse plays; *The Gallant Cassian,* one of Arthur Schnitzler's *Marionettenspiele,* which, albeit with live Interplayers, could have almost reprised the puppet shows Kees produced with and for his friends; and *The Tenor* by Frank Wedekind. The Wedekind, however, was soon substituted by an original play, *The Brimstone Butterfly,* by Kees's partner in the Showcase, Michael Grieg.

Michael Grieg, Nina Boas, Weldon Kees, and Penny Vieregge, the Showplace stage, May 1955.

Four Times One was to premier on Friday, May 20, but the need to rehearse the four plays obliged Kees to reschedule for May 27. Then, the day before the opening, a surprise fire department inspection closed the Showplace. The cost of bringing the building up to code forced Kees to cancel. "The fire department's final dicta involved sheet-rocking The Showplace practically down to the faucets in the lavatory," he wrote to the actor and teacher Byron Bryant in early June, "the towel, clutched compulsively for so long, has now been thrown in."

Unlike the B-picture vernacular of Kees's screen stories, *The Waiting Room* is existentialist theater, showing the influence of Samuel Beckett's *Waiting for Godot* and Jean Paul Sartre's *No Exit*. The piece has an American flavor and point of view in keeping with the social commentary and pathos of William Inge, Tennessee Williams, and Carson McCullers. Of course, Kees did not have to borrow from them too much since his poetry had covered much of the same ground in separating the American psyche from the American dream. Nowhere is this better represented than in the play's final speech, which alludes to Vincent Youmans' 1925 Broadway musical *No, No Nanette* and its hit song, "I Want to Be Happy." Such ironies, especially from the popular culture that pretended to offer an escape from life's entrapments, are part of Kees's vernacular of disappointment and social critique — like finding "There's a Small Hotel" in one of his Robinson poems. That same vernacular is in Kees's paintings and collages, the latter often using snatches of newspaper headlines, not unlike the one Jill reads early in *The Waiting Room*. Kees's desire to protest Eisenhower's America is evident in his marginal notes for the play, where he considered having Nancy madly recite "The Pledge of Allegiance." Yet, as Kees perfected how Nina was to mentally disintegrate, the discipline of staging a play fell apart in the days before *The Waiting Room* would have its premiere. To Jan Davis, the actress who played Jill, not only did the production seem unprofessional on Kees's part, but no longer impersonal, too. It seemed, on hindsight, to be a distress signal:

> The rehearsals were undisciplined, chaotic. I was uncomfortable, for however messy my emotional life was, I was trained by pros in the theatre. I asked Weldon: please could we start on time, and have rehearsal plans. Weldon

was depressed, talked of suicide . . . Nobody picked up on the deep despair that was driving him.

In the years after Kees's disappearance, these actors and a handful of Kees's friends were the only ones who knew anything about the play's existence or if it existed in a finished form. Eventually, the play came to the attention of the poet Kenneth Rexroth, who may have actually read a finished copy. In his review of Kees's *Collected Poems* in the Sunday *New York Times* of January 8, 1961, Rexroth wrote:

> Besides these moving poems, Weldon Kees left behind an excellent play of the type now most successful off-Broadway, called "The Waiting Room." I hope his heirs will make it available soon. Like his poems, it was just a few years too early.

Postcard announcement for the premiere of *Four Times One.*

Soon after the publication of this review, Kees's father, John Kees, the trustee of his son's literary estate, received requests to read the play from New Horizons Productions and Jullis Productions (off-Broadway theater groups), WCBS-TV's *New York Forum,* and an independent producer, John C. Fleming. Lacking a final draft of the play, the elder Kees pieced together his son's "Director's copy," a working draft. Thus, John Kees bridged gaps in scenes and left in the continuity problems that Weldon Kees had not resolved in the director's copy, such as "killing off" the first balloon in the play, which Nancy holds on a stick, and the one she inflates out of nowhere at the end of the play. Nancy, too, had to "fill" Jill's shoes. For that, Kees would had to have Nina Boas perform barefoot — as she appears in a *San Francisco Chronicle* photograph mopping the Showplace's floor.

John Kees circulated *The Waiting Room* to those who had requested it. He sought out others, too, whose venues seemed appropriate for noncommercial plays, such as Norris Houghton of the Phoenix Theater in New York. But, the manuscript was politely returned with varying degrees of encouragement. "I don't mean to damn it with faint praise at all," the television director Paul Melton wrote the elder Kees in a typical letter, "but the two words that occur to me to describe it are interesting and amusing." Kees also sent the play to the American Literary Exchange, but the agency refused to represent the work of a playwright soon to be declared legally dead. *The Waiting Room* was eventually premiered in October 1988, as part of a Kees symposium held in Beatrice, Nebraska. The actors, all from a dinner theater troupe, performed in the dining room of the town's Best Western Motel. Later, the manuscript of the director's copy was published both in *Prairie Schooner* and in a fine press edition. What follows is a different text.

While researching *Vanished Act,* I discovered an incomplete copy *The Waiting Room* in a cache of Kees's papers that had once been in the possession of Michael Grieg. It revealed that the stage version had been revised into a teleplay. Since Kees did not mention such a production in any of his writings, I date the production of the teleplay to those weeks between the closure of the Showplace and Kees's disappearance on July 18, 1955. Comparing it to the director's copy, the teleplay is, in all likelihood, based on the most finished version. However, the teleplay itself is missing pages and this required a judicious reconstruction using the director's copy to fill in the omitted pages at the end of the play. I have also incorporated Kees's typed and handwritten corrections to further approximate a finished play and to minimize any emendations on my part. In addition to the technical differences of a play for television and a stage play, there are textual differences. The director's copy originally has Nancy recite "The Hardy Garden" by Edna St. Vincent

Millay. It surely entailed permission and copyright fees that Kees got around by supplying his own Millay-like verse.

I consider that poem, a product of Kees's third way, to be his last.

The Waiting Room
A Teleplay

JILL: *Willis used to say — my God! — that there was a tribe in Australia where the mothers eat their children.*

PATRICIA: *Not only in Australia.*

— Lines added and struck out of the Director's copy

For Nina Boas, Jan Davis, and Penny Vieregge[1]

Cast

Nancy, a woman of 23

Jill, a woman of 40

Patricia, a woman of 35

Nancy's Mother

Nancy's Father

Man with a Cigar

Shackelton

A bare stage, except for two benches of the kind used in bus and railway stations. Lights up slowly: harsh intense day. Seated on the bench at right, Patricia; on the bench at left, Jill. Jill looking through a newspaper; Patricia has a magazine in her lap. Jill looks appraisingly at Patricia; goes back to her paper. Patricia looks curiously at Jill as Nancy enters. Nancy carries a book and a balloon on a stick. She starts over to the bench on which Jill is sitting, but Jill looks up suddenly and gives her a look that intimidates her. Nancy sits down on the bench with Patricia, who looks curiously at the balloon.

NANCY: I got it for my little boy. He and his father are meeting me here.

JILL: (*Feels her face; reads from the paper*) "Dear Alice Hooper Maxwell: I have been going with a man for twenty-two years. I am fifty and he is ten years older than I am, and he has a wife and five children. They live in another city, but he is on the road a lot — a traveling man. For twenty-two years he has been promising me that he'll divorce his wife and marry me. What would you do, Mrs. Maxwell, in my position?" (*Looks up, exasperated*) Oh, for — (*Lights a cigarette nervously; to Patricia*) Do you have the time?

PATRICIA: Sorry.

JILL: (*To Nancy*): Do you know what time it is?

NANCY: Why, it's — why, look, my watch has stopped. (*Shakes her wrist*)

JILL: I wish I knew what time it was. (*To herself while other girls read*) Did I leave that oven on? I'm always leaving that oven on. It went out that time when I went to see *Carmen Jones*[2] with Philip and when we got home the parakeets were dead . . . I must have turned it out, though . . . I remember . . . I keep remembering how they looked, with their claws, there at the bottom of their cage, and the newspaper at the bottom of the cage had part of a headline: Foresees Prosperous Future For . . .

PATRICIA: (*Reading from magazine, satirically*) "The all-in-one suit, in both tweed and flannel. Once it's unjacketed you see its core (*Lifts eyebrows in mock astonishment*) — a bare, squared camisole in the same fabric. From Carol Mahon." Why didn't someone think of this sooner?

JILL: People are dense.

NANCY: There are some poems that always make me want to cry. Do either of you care for poetry?

JILL: Oh, if there's anything I hate, it's waiting. Waiting for people, waiting for something to happen, waiting for something not to happen . . .

NANCY: Listen.

> *I have lost my way in the forest, O my beloved,*
> *Mist has obscured your face.*
> *The trees waver like weeds that are seen through water;*
> *There is fear in this place.*
>
> *I have forgotten the dark paths of the mind*
> *And the terrible red canopy of the heart;*
> *I am a child or the pale ghost of a child,*
> *Strangely withdrawn and apart.*

If I should touch your lips in this dim forest,
  I should perish of cold and fall down slain.
Here there is no sound but fungus dripping
  Through fog, like a slow rain.

Somewhere there are bells drowned in a pool;
  They ring when the pool is stirred.
Let the woods close in upon me and the night fall.
  Leave me without a word.[3]

Isn't that beautiful?

JILL: We came in the door and all the lights were out and Phillip said, "Oh, my God you've left the oven on again!" As if he never made a mistake in his life. What about the time he got the case of Scotch from a client of his in the South and left it out there in the hallway? I always thought those two boys who live across the hall are the ones who stole it. Twelve quarts of Dewar's White Label . . . "Oh my God you've left the oven on!" he said. As if . . .

PATRICIA: (*Sliding down in the bench*) I always have trouble staying on these things.

NANCY: Have you been waiting long?

PATRICIA: I dunno. It just seems long. I liked the way you read that poem. I never read poetry, but it sounded good — the way you read it.

(*A man with a cigar approaches the women, pauses, sits down on bench by Nancy, looks her over. He leans down toward her and whispers in her ear. Nancy draws away from him; he persists.*)

NANCY: Go away! Go away! Leave me alone.

(*He is unruffled and whispers some more*)

PATRICIA: Leave the kid alone! (*Stands up*) She doesn't have to listen to you if she doesn't want to! (*He grins and blows smoke in her face, looks back at Nancy and walks away*)

NANCY: Thank you.

PATRICIA: What a nerve. When I was in the nightclub circuit —

NANCY: You were on the stage?

PATRICIA: For fifteen years.

NANCY: Isn't that wonderful! I don't think . . . I know — I've never met an actress before in my life. When I was in high school . . . I wanted to be an actress. I saw Ingrid Bergman in a picture.

JILL: With Humphrey Bogart.

NANCY: She was so beautiful . . . (To *Patricia*) Were you really on the stage'?

PATRICIA: Stock, musicals in New York, vaudeville, nightclubs, road companies . . . the works.

NANCY: How did you get started?

PATRICIA: Well, there was this man — (*Does a double take; laughs*) Talent, naturally, talent! No, honestly, it was my dear old mother. Dear old mother, my foot. She was one of those real shoving, pushing, ruthless ambitious women that missed the boat and wanted to get their daughters on another one. She started me on ballet the minute I was able to stand without holding on to something. You know. (*Patricia gets up and imitates a little girl learning ballet steps*) And then — swiftly up the ladder of success!

JILL: (*Looking away from the other two*) It's stuffy in here. (*The other two look at her*) Oh, I beg your pardon.

PATRICIA: Oh, that's all right. Ladder of success, my foot. My first big performance after Mother got me to New York was putting pieces of huckleberry pie in the compartments at Horn and Hardart's.

NANCY: Horn and Hardart's?

PATRICIA: You know, the automat. Oh, you don't know? Mother left my father, who drank, and, boy, did he have reasons to.

NANCY: I had a wonderful father.

(*Dissolve to* NANCY'S FATHER *in a white surgeon's coat. He stands rigidly for a moment, then shakes a thermometer.*[4])

NANCY: Daddy was a doctor. (*Very confidentially*) He specialized in female complaints.

PATRICIA: I've had a couple of 'em in my day.

NANCY: We lived in Santa Barbara. But . . . it was like your father: he drank, too.

(NANCY'S FATHER *takes a flask from his hip pocket, drinks, looks warily around.*)

NANCY: Mother was always calling him up on the phone.

(FATHER *picks up phone*)

NANCY: "What are you doing now, Charlie?" she'd say — my father's name was Charlie — "What are you doing now? Did you get rid of that secretary of yours like I told you to? I'm positive you're drinking again, in spite of everything I've told you. What are you doing, Charlie, what are you doing?"

(FATHER *hangs up, has another drink*)

PATRICIA: Poor man.

NANCY: He's dead now. (*Dissolve out on Father*)

PATRICIA: (*Touched*) Oh, I'm sorry.

NANCY: (*Rapidly*) You know? After one of those phone calls one day, he hung up the receiver and . . . shot himself. (*A long pause*)

JILL: (*Anxious, tense*) Listen, did you hear that sound?

PATRICIA: I didn't hear anything.

JILL: (*To Nancy*) Didn't you hear it?

NANCY: No.

JILL: It was like . . . something falling.

(*A long pause.* PATRICIA *and* NANCY *look at each other, puzzled.* JILL *very nervous, listening.*)

PATRICIA: (*As though to break the tension*) Well. About my career on the Great White Way. Mother and I had a fight and she went back to South Bend — for a while. I lost my job. I auditioned all the time for chorus jobs. I was so low. I was living in the most terrible hotel on West 45th Street where the manager had designs on me . . .

NANCY: (*Yearningly*) David, David. (*Stands, walks forward. Speaks: entirely internal*) There aren't many men these days that are really considerate . . . and good. He used to call me from the office, after we were married, twice a day; I always knew where he was, what he was doing . . .

JILL: (*Gets up, pacing around the room*) He's not coming. He's lying again. All those weeks I was flat on my back in the hospital . . . I was good . . . I was! I was! I did everything he wanted, everything! Even that time he mixed it up with that Mrs. Jamison . . . I didn't even raise my voice (*Loudly*) I didn't even raise my voice! (*Sits down, crosses her legs, then wearily*) Like hell I didn't. Sometimes I think the whole thing came about through some biological mix-up. Willis used to get drunk and talk about that. "Jill," he'd say — I remember he used to lean forward as though it was a matter of life and death, and he'd point his finger at me . . . God, he never

82

cleaned his fingernails . . . and he'd say, "In this culture" — he was always using that phrase. I wanted to simply scream sometimes, he said it so often . . . "In this culture the women are so mixed up they don't know what they want any more . . . they don't even know what they are . . ." (*Pause*) Those fingernails of his looked as though he dipped them regularly in india ink . . . He carried the whole thing too far, of course. It's all perfectly clear what we want: money, security, a man . . . lots of men.

PATRICIA: (*With magazine: to Nancy; she points to a picture*) Look at this little tomato. I used to look like that . . . ten years ago . . . Well I was telling you. I was living in this fleabag in New York and I couldn't get anything. I'm not kidding. I was at the point of taking up a life of shame. And then there was one of those things that happen sometimes. I started to tell you about this man, Bert Shackelton . . .

(*Dissolve through to* SHACKLETON *sitting at his desk with his feet up, reading 'Variety'*)

PATRICIA: Well, he turned out to be one of the most unusual men in the world — an honest agent. (SHACKLETON *assumes an expression of absolute rectitude*) Well, honest most of the time.

(SHACKLETON *looks as though he was scheming up something*)

JILL: There isn't even a telephone in this place.

PATRICIA: He had a hole in the wall off Times Square. When I first met him he didn't have dime one.

(SHACKLETON *pulls out empty pants pockets*)

PATRICIA: But he was pretty wonderful. I showed him my many talents.

(PATRICIA *appears at Shackelton's desk, pantomimes various things: a fashion model, a great lady, a Charleston dancer.* SHACKLETON *watches her with deep interest.*)

PATRICIA: I could see that he was interested . . . Well, to make a long story even longer, he began getting me jobs. Nothing very big at first.

(*Dissolve out on* SHACKLETON)

PATRICIA: I was all over the Sears, Roebuck catalog one year . . . there was a photograph of me modeling winter underwear for the farm trade. Buttoned down the front, snug as a bug, where it counts. I got into the chorus line of a show called "Emma's Dilemma" . . . awful. (*Holds her nose*) It closed out of town, never hit New York. "Emma's Dilemma" — it was a musical version of *Madame Bovary*.

(NANCY *is staring at the balloon, turning it as if it were a crystal ball. It deflates.*[5])

JILL: Say, have you ever overheard men talking about women? It's perfectly disgusting. One time I was out in the kitchen baking a deep-dish blueberry pie — Willis loved a deep-dish blueberry pie — and he and some friend of his were in the living room drinking scotch on the rocks. And I mean drinking. This friend of his taught theosophy or something equally idiotic at some dinky little college back East. Well, I overheard them . . . I heard Willis saying, "I can't figure them out any more; just can't figure them out. Why, that one out in the kitchen — " He was talking about me, mind you — Well, never mind what he said.

PATRICIA: Go on. I'm interested.

JILL: Well, he said to this man — a terrible little man who kept wrinkling up his nose as though he was trying to get something out of it — he said that they ought to go around with little tags pinned on them — he was talking about women — "little tags on them like at conventions." He said that one could have a tag that said, "I'm a frigid, selfish little bitch" and another would have a tag that would say "Watch out for some hairpulling after I've had five martinis," and another one would say, "All I want is my career and your money . . ." Willis and those friends of his!

PATRICIA: Men would read those little tags and it wouldn't make the least bit of difference.

JILL: (*Paces around room*) Jealousy, that's what's the trouble. And don't let anyone tell you men aren't just as bad as women. Willis and his "culture" and all his ideas . . . He was just as bad as the rest of them when it came to jealousy. Oh, at the beginning they're full of honey and promises. At the beginning, Willis used to say, "If there's one thing I pride myself on, it's that I don't have a jealous bone in my body." (*To Patricia*) Why do you suppose there isn't even a telephone in this place? What if someone wanted to make a phone call?

PATRICIA: They'd be in a bad way, wouldn't they?

JILL: These shoes are killing me.

PATRICIA: (*To Nancy, as* JILL *kicks off shoes and sits down on the bench next to Patricia*) Well, to get back to Bert. In a year or two I was getting some pretty darn good parts in musicals; it really set him up . . . Ten years on Broadway . . . (*Pause. During the last few speeches, since her last speech, Nancy has been staring intently at Jill.*)

NANCY: Why did you let me grow up?
(PATRICIA *alert;* JILL *nervous and annoyed*)

NANCY: (*Toneless*) I said: why did you let me grow up? Why didn't you tell me about the ward with the flying beds in it and that nurse with a face like a . . . (*Rubs her hands piteously across her face*)

JILL: If you think I —

PATRICIA: (*Abruptly to Jill*) Now just hold it. (*To Nancy, patiently*) That's all right, honey. Tell me all about it. I've seen plenty of beds flying around in my time.

NANCY: (*Trying hard to think*) It's ... not ... right growing up. I go back over it all the time and try to ... (*She stands up and walks rigidly, semi-catatonic, to Jill*) Don't pretend you're not my mother. Those are my mother's shoes. When I was a little little girl ... the ignominy, he said, the i g n o m i n y of growing up ... growing up ... growing up. (*Nancy steps into Jill's shoes, walks around in them like a little girl.*[6] JILL *starts to get up;* PATRICIA *restrains her with her hand. Nancy singing like a little girl, posturing of a girl of ten, experiments with cosmetics: makes up mouth badly with lipstick.*)

(*Dissolve to Nancy alone in the room. Her pantomime continues. She is no longer wearing Jill's shoes. She dances, "whirling from one boy to another." She kisses a man and transforms into a "brisk, efficient secretary."*[7])

NANCY: (*At phone*[8]) Bullock, Masterson and Ives. No, I'm sorry, Mrs. Ives, Mr. Ives has not come in yet this morning ... Yes, I'll tell him. Bullock, Masterson and Ives. .... He's on another line, do you mind waiting? (NANCY *freezes as if remembering*)

(*Like an apparition that no one else can see, Nancy's Mother, a real horror, enters the waiting room and walks up behind Nancy.*)

MOTHER: (*to Nancy, rigid, frozen*) I held you in my arms when you were a tiny baby. (*She eyes Nancy*) Heaven knows I tried to bring you up to be a decent wholesome girl. (*Picks up phone*) What are you doing, Charlie? What are you up to down at that office? Last night I smelled whiskey on your breath again. And last night I'm sure I detected cigarette smoke on Nancy's breath when she came in from her (*Contemptuously*) date. She didn't want to kiss her mother goodnight, that much was obvious. What are you doing down there, Charlie? Hello, hello. Oh, you have a patient. Well. (*Hangs up phone*) It's wrong to let any man so much as touch you until the day comes when you're a married woman. (NANCY *sits back down and sinks into her bench. She puts her head in her hands and*

86

sobs.) You never really liked that beautiful doll I bought you on your second birthday, did you? I ordered it especially out of the mail-order catalogue. You always preferred that filthy old rag thing instead, taking it to bed with you. (*Quick shift in tempo*) You know I love you, dear; you know I love you more than life itself. (*Slower*) And those puppies you used to bring into the house! You know I can't stand animals underneath my feet, and the dirt . . . and you can get diseases from cats and dogs. (*Sits down by Nancy, who turns her face away, sweetly*) You're twelve years old now and I want to have a heart-to-heart talk with my little girl. (*Puts hand on Nancy's hand*) Oh, I don't know whether I can bring myself to say these things to you or not. Men are — well. My own mother never told me anything. (*Pause, then sharply*) You've got to always remember that in this life you can't be too careful, and I mean about everything; you must learn to watch every penny, as I've had to do, always keep your distance dear, your mother knows what she's talking about, it's disgraceful the way your father has spent money like a drunken sailor — sometimes I think it's only prayer that has given me the courage to go on — you've got to think of yourself first if you're going to get anywhere in the world. And learn to know the right people, good church people, always go to church on Sunday, you didn't wash the back of your neck again, in this world, in this world, in this world you can't be too careful, you can't be too careful, you can't be —

(NANCY *screams. Then clicking noises like a cracked phonograph record.*)

(*Dissolve to Nancy in the waiting room with Patricia next to her on the bench in place of Mother. Jill is in the facing bench. Her shoes are back on her feet.* NANCY *sobs.* PATRICIA *tries to comfort her; she shakes her off.*)

JILL: She's hysterical. Oh, it's all so idiotic . . . the jealousy, the bitching, the faking, all the other things we do. For love. For what they call love. Happiness. Be happy. Whatever that means. (*Starts suddenly*) Listen, didn't you hear that?

PATRICIA: (*Decisively*) No, I didn't hear a thing. Look, we've got to do something about this one.

JILL: Oh, she'll get over it. (*Sits listening*) I heard a sound like something in the wind — a window shade — something — blowing.

PATRICIA: You heard what?

JILL: There's a sound, you hear a sound, late, late at night you come out of a sound sleep and I heard that noise in the next room where Willis — (*Catches herself*) Love. I got to the point where I was (*Stronger*) in love with jealousy. I don't even know why. I was wild with it. I was playing two men against each other for everything I could. It would be late, late at night . . . I was living in New York. One would call me up . . . the phone would ring . . . and I'd be in bed with the other one. I could feel his jealousy on the back of my neck and the other one's jealousy coming over the phone like a red-hot wire. I didn't even think of it as jealousy. I just thought . . . me — me — me.

PATRICIA: (*Very husky, her brassiness is all gone*) Bert, Bert Shackelton. He was the only guy I really loved, with all my heart. And he never even made a pass at me. He had a wife. If I could have . . . If I could have just managed to get him to see me in a different way . . . You know how it is when you're walking all alone down a street that you know just as well as the back of your hand, and all of a sudden you see the side of a building or a window or a footprint in the sidewalk that you'd never realized was there . . . I don't know: Bert was . . . Bert always looked at me as if I were a thing . . . you know? A sort of commodity — a nice commodity, of course — blood in my veins, but a . . . commodity. Maybe he was just protecting himself . . . (*Looks around*) There was that day when we were in Philadelphia together, and he came into my hotel room. God, it was hot, I remember an electric fan whining and that terrible wallpaper with roses . . . I knew what I wanted . . . I knew just what to do . . . I could have done it and in no time we'd have been . . . (*Long pause*) I couldn't do it. I couldn't do it to him.

88

JILL: (*Looking at her face in her compact*) My God! I'm getting to look like my mother.

NANCY: (*Looking up, wild*) You are my mother; you are my mother.

JILL: Am I?

NANCY: (*Comes over to Jill*) You don't mean to tell me you don't remember. All those months after David was killed . . . you don't remember. You don't remember . . . You don't want to remember (*Shakes Jill*) You don't! You don't. In the hospital, you kept telling me you wouldn't let them give me shock therapy. I was sitting there with my world all gone like a punctured balloon. My face was pressed against the wall and the doctor had a face like my father's. You kept saying, "How much is this going to cost, Doctor?" And "did he think my little girl will ever be well again?" And how you couldn't understand how a daughter of yours . . . (*Pause*) My nose was so hard against the wall I thought the bone in it was going to break. And I felt myself . . . something so private and deep and far inside me go down like a death. Like David the night they brought him back, all smashed up and burned. He'd been out with another girl and they were both drunk and on the highway . . .

JILL: (*Stands up*) Stop it! Stop it!

PATRICIA: Let her get it out, for God's sake! Let her get it out!

NANCY: You killed him! You killed him! You always wanted him dead. You killed everything I loved! (*Slumps down on floor* No, no, no. (JILL *and* PATRICIA *look at each other*) I was there with you at the clinic and I felt — It was like something breaking, I am trying to think, like that time we were high up in an office building, David and I, and there was a parade and people were cheering about something and I saw a piece of paper go down and then the wind caught it and tore it and it ripped apart — (*Sobs*)

PATRICIA: It'll be all right now. It'll be all right now. (*She comforts Nancy*)

JILL: People can't say what they want to to each other any more. I remember Willis saying (*With sympathy*), "In this culture — " pointing his finger of his right hand in my face — "In this culture, people are so busy chasing after money and position they don't stand a chance. They don't know how to live. They're raised on happiness, happiness, and optimism and getting ahead and then when the going gets rough, they can't take it. No wonder so many of them crack." (NANCY *suddenly looks up*)

(*Dissolve to* NANCY'S FATHER *on the other side of the waiting room.* NANCY *starts suddenly.*)

NANCY: (*Running over to Father*) I always loved you best of all. (*Dissolve out on* FATHER. *Nancy stands alone. Lost.*)

JILL: (*Face forward, staring*) At one time or another, I've believed just about anything and everything. And now I don't know what I believe in. I don't know if I even believe in men anymore.

PATRICIA: (*Rises from the bench and speaks to Nancy*) You've got to believe in something, even if it's the worst. (*She takes Nancy by the chin and lifts her head*) You ought to be wasteful . . . with love . . . with affection . . . don't think I don't know . . . we're not going to be around very long.

JILL: I wonder what time it is.

PATRICIA: I don't know, but I'm through with waiting. I'm not going to wait any more. (To *Nancy*) How about you, kid?

JILL: I'm coming with you.

NANCY: Sometimes nothing turns up and you have to live with that, too. I can still pretend. (*Does a quick spin movement of gaiety, of elation. Grins.*)

JILL: I'm hungry. (*To Nancy*) Are you coming?

(NANCY *stares at them in silence*)

PATRICIA: It's no use trying to make people do something they don't want to. Goodbye . . . I didn't catch your name. I'll remember the way you read that poem.

JILL: Starving. (*To Nancy*) Maybe whatever it is you're waiting for will happen. Goodbye. (*To Patricia*) Come on. I could eat a horse.

PATRICIA: We'll call a taxi?

JILL: Okay.

PATRICIA: (*To Nancy*) Look, take care of yourself.

(PATRICIA *and* JILL *exit.* NANCY *watches them intently as they go. There is a balloon on the bench before her. She picks it up, looks at it as if surprised and begins to blow it up. She holds it out admiringly.*)

NANCY: I want to be happy! I want to be happy! I want to be happy! (Breaks *the balloon. Drum roll and dissolve to epilogue on screen.*)

> And the home I scatter, and house I batter,
> Having first of all made the children fall,
> And he who felled them is never to know,
> He gave birth to each child that received the blow,
> Till, Madness, I am, have let him go.
>
> — Browning, "Aristophanes' Apology"

Notes

1. This dedication is taken from the flyers Kees printed for the opening of the stage version of the play.

2. The film *Carmen Jones* (1954) is a film adaptation of Bizet's opera, Carmen. It starred Dorothy Dandridge and Harry Belafonte and featured a cast of mainly African-American actors.

3. In the director's copy, Nancy recites Edna St. Vincent Millay's "The Hardy Garden."

4. In the final version of the play, Kees replaced different colored spotlights with camera dissolves (e.g., Nancy's father is lit in blue for this scene).

5. Kees had crossed out this necessary stage instruction in the director's copy, but left an arrow to indicate where it might be repositioned.

6. There is no stage direction for Nancy to remove her own shoes or put them back on.

7. The director's copy lacks this second phase of the pantomime, which has been edited for continuity here; it takes up with the Mother's speech instead.

8. This is still part of Nancy's pantomime, not a prop.